97

St. Louis Community College

Forest Park
Florissant Valley
Meramec

Instructional Resources
St. Louis, Missouri

GAYLORD

Mexican Cinema/

Mexican Woman,

1940–1950

Latin American Communication and Popular Culture
Series Editors
Harold E. Hinds, Jr., and Charles M. Tatum

MEXICAN CINEMA/

MEXICAN WOMAN,

1940–1950

Joanne Hershfield

The University of Arizona Press
Tucson

∞ This book is printed on acid-free,
archival-quality paper
Manufactured in the
United States of America
First printing

Library of Congress
Cataloging-in-Publication Data
Hershfield, Joanne, 1950–
Mexican cinema/Mexican woman, 1940–1950 / Joanne Hershfield.
p.   cm. — (Latin American communication and popular culture)
Includes bibliographical references (p.) and index.
ISBN 0-8165-1636-7 (cloth : acid-free paper).
— ISBN 0-8165-1637-5 (pbk. : acid-free paper)
1. Motion pictures—Mexico—History.   2. Women in motion pictures.
I. Title.   II. Series.
PN1993.5.M4H38   1996
791.43'652042'0972—dc20   96-10110
CIP

British Cataloguing-in-Publication Data
A catalogue record
for this book is available
from the British Library.

Publication of this book is made possible in part by the proceeds of a
permanent endowment created with the assistance of a Challenge Grant
from the National Endowment for the Humanities, a federal agency.

For my grandmother,

Rose Hershfield

(1904–1993)

CONTENTS

LIST OF ILLUSTRATIONS

ACKNOWLEDGMENTS

This book emerged out of my dissertation work in the Department of Radio-Television-Film at the University of Texas at Austin. I want to thank my adviser, Professor Charles Ramirez Berg, who initiated my interest in Mexican cinema and has sustained and encouraged me in numerous ways throughout my career. I am also grateful to Janet Staiger, Mary Desjardins, and Thomas Schatz, not only for their thorough and critical readings of various versions of the dissertation, but also for what I have learned from them.

Others at the University of Texas at Austin who supported and advised me include Emile McAnany, Sharon Strover, Henry Selby, and Ted Gordon; I extend my appreciation to these professors. I would also like to thank the College of Communication at the University of Texas at Austin for providing me with a grant to conduct research in Mexico, and Kathryn Burger and Lillian Respress for easing my passage over various bureaucratic hurdles.

Many more people contributed to the preparation and completion of this book. I would especially like to thank two scholars of Mexican film, Julianne Burton-Carvajal and David Maciel, for their advice and encouragement. Thanks also to Ivan Trujillo and his staff at the Dirección General de Actividades Cinematográficas de la UNAM in Mexico City, who provided me access to their archives and gave me permission to reprint numerous stills for this book. My colleagues Jacqueline Bobo and Lucila Vargas offered scholarly and moral encouragement in the face of daily stress. At the University of Arizona Press, I would like to thank my editor, Joanne O'Hare, for her confidence in the book, and my copy editor, Beth Wilson, for her careful attention to detail.

I am indebted to my family: my parents, Syd and Sally Hershfield; my sister, Rochelle Hershfield; my brother, Paul Hershfield; and my father-in-law, Lyman R. Fink. They have always believed in me and supported my varied endeavors. Most of all, I thank Jim and Gillian for reminding me to come out and play, and for their love, which continues to enrich my life in unbelievable ways.

Mexican Cinema/
Mexican Woman,
1940-1950

INTRODUCTION

Mexican Cinema/Mexican Woman, 1940–1950 concentrates on a narrow moment in the history of Mexican film in order to investigate the ways in which the cinematic figure of woman functioned to mediate narrative and social debates. Through an examination of six women-centered melodramas from the 1940s—*María Candelaria* (Emilio Fernández, 1943), *Río Escondido* (Emilio Fernández, 1947), *Distinto amanecer* (Julio Bracho, 1943), *Salón México* (Emilio Fernández, 1948), *Doña Bárbara* (Fernando de Fuentes, 1943), and *Susana* (*Carne y demonio;* Luis Buñuel, 1950)—I show how woman, as an already existing sign of ambiguity in Mexican culture (virgin/whore, mother/femme fatale, nurturer/destroyer), served as a ready-made symbol of the instability of social and sexual relations in Mexico in the 1940s. It will be seen that the above mechanisms did not emerge full-blown in the 1940s but may be traced to earlier representations grounded in historical legend and cultural myths.

The work of the Mexican painter Frida Kahlo, whose career spanned the 1930s and 1940s, has been heralded for its depiction of woman's divided "inner" nature. Sarah M. Lowe, for instance, finds that Kahlo's self-portraits—which variously portrayed the artist as a mother, the Virgin, an Indian, a mestiza, or a man—represent a "fusion of a public with a private self" through their exploration of "her condition as Mexican, as woman, and as disabled in relation to each other" (1993, 34). Jean Franco points out, however, that Kahlo's repeated portrayals of woman's naked body "penetrated by technology" are not merely representations of the individual self but a "socialized body . . . controlled by modern society" (1989, 107).

In *The Broken Column*, painted in 1944, Kahlo depicts her own naked torso, constrained by a steel corset and split in half by a phallic column rising out of her loins. If this female image is at once an object of desire, a site of reproduction, and a broken woman's body, it is also a symbol of a female social subject conscious of the fact that she has been violated and regulated by the technological arm of patriarchal society. Hayden Herrera (1983), examining Kahlo's representations of duality, suggests that the artist's concentration on self-portraits not only "accentuated Frida's sense of having two identities" but also forced Kahlo to approach self-representation as a firmly divided subject.

Films in the 1940s reproduced this divided subject, portraying women as virtuous and suffering mothers, seduced and abandoned young girls, and outright *mala mujeres* (bad women). However, the significance of these filmic representations is that, unlike Kahlo's paintings or women's literature, the cinema, as a mass medium that did not require a cultural literacy, was able to "represent and transmit to a population that literature had never reached" new ideologies of family, nation, and sexual difference (Franco, 1989, xx).

Previous Histories

Mexican cinema flourished, and audiences flocked to the cinema throughout the 1940s. By 1948 there were approximately 2.5 million cinema tickets sold each week in about 1,300 theaters (de Usabel, 1982, 207). Although the foreign share of the Mexican market still accounted for 75 percent of these admissions, Mexico was producing more films than any other Latin American nation. Despite the historical dominance of Hollywood, Mexican cinema was able to achieve a level of economic, artistic, and popular success in the 1940s that was unprecedented in any other Latin American country.

This accomplishment was due to both internal and external factors: the international crisis of World War II, the development of an unprecedented economic independence, the institution of supportive state protectionist policies, the success of Mexican films in other Latin American countries, and what Carlos Monsiváis describes as "an alliance between the film industry and the audiences of the faithful, between the films and the communities that saw themselves represented there." This alliance worked to support new discourses of national identity. According to Monsiváis, the cinema screen did not merely represent dreams and fantasies for recently urbanized and largely illiterate Mexican audiences; these audiences saw the films as reflections and explanations of their own reality. Monsiváis argues that Mexican cinema thus was able to transform and reshape popular culture and national identity (1993, 142–144).

For Monsiváis, the authority of cinema as a shaper of national identity lies not in the fact that it reflects society. Instead, cinema's power to remake culture in the image of the "nation" persists because it is able to dramatize social problems and relations in a language that makes culture intelligible to its audiences. In addition to interpreting culture, cinema functions as an efficient "structure of mediation" that works to legitimate unequal relations of political power.[1]

According to Fredric Jameson, structural mediations operate as interventions among different levels of reality: the social, the psychic, and the narrative levels of cultural histories. While acknowledging the relative autonomy of each of these levels, Jameson argues that it is possible to conceive of a structural relation based on a notion of totality. Whereas classical Marxist analyses worked to "seek a unified meaning to which the various levels and components of the work contribute in a hierarchical way," Jameson's intent is to "[explode] the seemingly unified text into a host of clashing and contradictory elements" (1991, 56). Mediation is a useful analytic tool, Jameson suggests, because it allows the critic to "analyze and articulate" two distinct structural levels of narrative, the ideological level and the textual level, in order to provide a "momentary reunification" of the "various regions of social life" represented in a text (1991, 40).

The Mexican scholar Roger Bartra sees the mediating function of cinema and other forms of popular culture in Mexico as "imaginary power-networks that define socially accepted forms of subjectivity and that are customarily considered as the fullest expression of national culture." In Bartra's view, popular culture does not merely reproduce social reality; it produces and legitimizes existing relations of power. Bartra goes on to suggest that through practices of popular and mass culture—cinema, radio, television, the press, speeches, and songs—the subjects of these practices, the popular audiences, "become actors, and the subjectivity is transformed into theater." For Bartra, cinema re-creates reality and "gives unity to the nation" (1992, 2–3). In this way, films function much as historical myths do: to provide singular, linear, and unbroken chains of meaning to historical subjects divided by material relations of class, ethnicity, and gender.

Mexican film historians have provided extensive as well as intensive chronologies of the history of Mexican cinema. Emilio García Riera's multivolume history of Mexican cinema, *Historia documental del cine mexicano, 1926–1966,* remains the most complete version of Mexican film history; Jorge Ayala Blanco's *La aventura del cine mexicano* traces the major themes and genres of Mexican cinema from the early silent cinema through the 1960s; Alejandro Rozado has written a number of essays on the director Emilio Fernández, collected in his *Cine y realidad social en México;* and the Mexican feminist historian and sociologist Julia Tuñón has broadly described the representation of women in the classical Mexican cinema in her two-volume dissertation, *Mujeres de luz y sombra: la construcción masculina de una imagen (1939–1952).* In addition, the work of other writers, such as Aurelio de los Reyes, Eduardo de la Vega, and Gustavo García, has provided Spanish-speaking readers with a broad spectrum of books and articles on the aesthetic, social, and political context of the Mexican film industry.

English-language studies of Mexican film, on the other hand, often situated in the context of the social and economic development of Latin American film in general, offer rather condensed versions of Mexican film history. These brief analyses tend to gloss over the relation between politics and artistic practices, and between ideological and cultural discourses. More important for this study, none of these works offers any sustained discussion or analysis of gender. Instead, they focus predominantly on economic issues of production and distribution while grounding their findings within a global perspective of industrial development. Jorge Schnitman, for example, argues that the foreign domination of local markets was the fundamental factor influencing "choice of content and the overall organization of film as a cultural form" in Latin America (1984, 8). Roy Armes's critical examination of the relation between culture and politics in Latin American cinema in his *Third World Filmmaking and the West* is necessarily broadly focused, given that, in the same volume, he is also considering national cinemas in India, East and Southeast Asia, the Middle East, and Africa, as well as discussing individual auteurs from each of these regions. Conversely, although Carl J. Mora's *Mexican Cinema: Reflections of a Society, 1896–1988* provides a more expanded survey of the history of Mexican cinema, it lacks a critical perspective on the relation between film and society.

Charles Ramirez Berg's *Cinema of Solitude: A Critical Study of Mexican*

Film, 1967–1983 differs significantly from most English-language studies of Mexican cinema. His book confirms Mexican cinema as a vibrant national cinema with roots in Mexican political, aesthetic, and cultural practices. Although *Cinema of Solitude* focuses on the 1970s, it does lay a foundation in Anglo-American film scholarship for understanding the origins of the classical style in Mexico as well as the relation between Mexican cinema and the woman question.[2]

According to Ramirez Berg, the classical Mexican cinema adhered to the narrative paradigm of the classical Hollywood film, which he defines as being constituted by a linear narrative trajectory and an omniscient, highly communicative, and moderately self-conscious narrative. Mexican scholars also point to Mexican cinema's debt to Hollywood. Monsiváis declares that "the founding enterprise of Mexican Cinema . . . is the 'nationalization' of Hollywood," noting that many Mexican stars, directors, and film technicians were trained in Hollywood, and that many Hollywood genres were assimilated into Mexican cinema (1993, 141). Given Mexico's geographical and political proximity to the United States, this cinematic interplay operated as a forceful presence in the development of Mexican cinema. However, what has not been as widely examined is the extent to which this influence was resisted.

Although Mexican films reproduced some features of the classical Hollywood paradigm, Mexico's Golden Age cinema was distinctly Mexican, telling Mexican stories and narrativizing Mexican social problems "in such a manner that Mexican ideology was made manifest. . . . It [Mexican cinema] adapted the Hollywood paradigm" to suit its own social and cultural needs (Ramirez Berg, 1992a, 16). Thus, although the Mexican film industry may have imported technology; industrial structures of production, exhibition, and distribution; raw materials; and stylistic and narrative strategies, Mexican filmmakers were able to forge a distinctly national cinema, one that finally gained international recognition during its Golden Age from 1935 through the early 1950s.

Social Contexts

The 1940s is often identified as the aesthetic and economic height of the Golden Age of Mexican cinema. The period was also one in which the social positions of women in Mexico were being reinterpreted within the postrevolutionary discourses of nationalism (which described the relations between the state and its subjects) and machismo (which similarly defined relations between men and women). On the one hand, women had been actively involved in the Mexican Revolution (1910–1920) as nurses, teachers, cooks, and *soldaderas* (female soldiers). After this protracted civil war, many women entered the expanding labor force as Mexico commenced a period of rapid industrialization and urbanization. On the other hand, the Revolution did not fundamentally alter the patriarchal structure of Mexican social life. Women were oppressed in new ways that emerged out of changing social discourses that subsequently generated new forms of cultural representations. Moreover, these new forms often reasserted older hierarchies based on sexual difference. This is because changes in social conditions do not immediately signal a shift in ideological conceptions of sexual roles and relations. Social crisis may provoke an effort by those in power to redefine identity—be it national or gendered—but these new identities often are built on existing paradigms. This was the case in postrevolutionary Mexico, when the construction of a new perception of the nation was a political priority and issues such as gender, class, and ethnicity intruded upon the various nationalist discourses and cultural practices, including cinema.

Mexican Cinema/Mexican Woman, 1940–1950 focuses on this junction of politics, gender, and aesthetics. The female figure serves as a productive site for exploring the conflicts surrounding social discourse because, as Judith Mayne puts it, "the female body does not always fit neatly into patterns of narrative, cinematic, or ideological opposition" (1989, 192). Woman's conspicuous sexuality threatens traditional concepts of femininity, while the demands of the classical narrative are often at odds with prevailing ideas about gender and gender roles.

The contradictions that lay at the heart of Mexican patriarchal ideology could not be held in check by social and cultural narratives about women and sexual difference. The portrayal of women in Mexican cinema in the 1940s served to reveal, and at the same time to problematize, the contradictory discourses surrounding the position of women in postrevolutionary Mexican family and social life. This volume focuses on the narrative and symbolic ways in which Mexican films exhibited those ideological conflicts surrounding gender and representation.

A number of other issues could be examined at this intersection of Mexican cinema, Mexican ideology, and narrative meaning. For example, the role of masculinity and the reconstruction of postrevolutionary patriarchy or the cinematic revision of the history of the Mexican Revolution might reveal similar social tensions. Likewise, a number of critical approaches, such as a genre study of the Mexican family melodrama, or an auteur analysis of a single director, such as Emilio "el Indio" Fernández, who directed more than fifteen films in the 1940s, would provide partial histories of the Mexican cinema in the 1940s.

As noted above, much of this work has already been done by Mexican film scholars and Mexican historians of film. This volume does not seek to "translate" the work of these Mexican scholars into English. Indeed, it should not be regarded as a descriptive history of Mexican cinema in the 1940s from a cross-cultural perspective. Instead, my study of the woman question in Mexican cinema is framed within a broad historical context that privileges the material basis of consciousness, experience, and the social construction of identity. This approach can be described as a criticism that understands "that the social and economic circumstances in which women and men live—the material conditions of their lives—are central to an understanding of culture and society" (Newton and Rosenfelt, 1985, xi). If such a method tends to focus on gender-specific relations of power, it also works to argue against an oppositional configuration that pits a monolithic, unchanging patriarchy against an essentialist notion of woman as a category that signifies oppression. Instead, a feminism grounded in the material reality of everyday experience recognizes multiple and historically specific forms of domination and resistance.

The following chapters are informed by feminist, historical, and psychoanalytic analyses of Hollywood and other national cinemas but seek to enlarge this body of work by exploring issues of the representation of woman as they relate to Mexican cinema of the 1940s. I argue that critics must pay attention to the historical, economic, and social conditions in which specific cinematic practices are produced, while at the same time recognizing that these contexts are not static, but are instead involved in continuous processes of transformation that must be considered in any cultural analysis.

Organization

In chapter 1, I look at the representation and function of female arche-types in Mexican history, focusing on two important mythohistorical figures, La Malinche and the Virgin of Guadalupe, who symbolize the Mexican version of the widely constructed polarity of woman—whore and virgin. Since the Spanish conquest of Mexico in the sixteenth cen-tury, the archetypal polarity of virgin/whore has been represented by La Malinche, the mistress of Cortés who became the symbol of the Spanish conquest of Mexico, and the Virgin of Guadalupe, an appari-tion of the Virgin Mary who appeared to a poor Indian man a few years after the conquest. In the narratives of Mexican myth and history, both of these figures are described within a contradictory sexual framework and are assigned a certain "use value" in terms of (re)productive pos-sibilities. La Malinche is represented as both mother (of the Mexican mestizo) and *la chingada*, the whore; the Virgin of Guadalupe is both Mother (of God) and virgin. In this chapter, I will be concerned both with the historical context of the emergence of each "sign of femi-ninity" and with the ways in which these signs have been recodified within Mexican social and cultural narrative discourses as functions of a constructed duality.

Chapter 2 traces the development of Mexican cinema as a national cinema and provides an institutional and cultural framework for under-standing the cinematic conventions and narrative structures that de-fined the films of the 1940s. I specifically discuss the ways in which film melodrama functioned to mediate ideology. The response of national cinemas to social crisis and the "woman question" is one area that has been looked at extensively in relation to melodrama.[3] Although Christine Gledhill expresses a certain wariness about what she refers to as the "ghettoization [of melodrama] as a woman's form," this avenue of investigation has proved fruitful for retheorizing female subjectivity, examining the cinematic representations of women, and reconsidering the function of woman in film narratives (1991, 207). More recently, film scholars are turning to other national cinema histories to identify both specific modes of representation and individual instances of the portrayals of woman within the context of the domestic sphere and the family in order to locate different relations between the woman on the screen and the woman in society.

Chapters 3 through 5 focus on issues of representation, narrative, and aesthetics in six Mexican films of the 1940s. In each chapter, I look at two films in the context of an overarching theme of national identity, relations between economics and gender, and the cultural and ideological constructions of sexual difference. Chapter 3 concentrates on the intersection of woman and national identity as represented in two films by Emilio Fernández: *María Candelaria* and *Río Escondido*. *María Candelaria*, a folkloric piece set in Mexico in the early 1900s, appears on one level to be a simple historical fable. On another level, however, it functions as a map of relations among sexual difference, class, and ethnicity in Mexico in the 1940s. *Río Escondido* provides a point of reference for the investigation of the relation between history, nation, and woman in postrevolutionary Mexico. The chapter also provides a context for a discussion of the classical Mexican cinematic style.

In chapter 4 I look at the Mexican *cabaretera* (dance-hall) film, a genre that opened a space to interrogate questions of economics, gender, and female sexual identity. The narrative strategy of Julio Bracho's *Distinto amanecer*, one of the early *cabaretera* films, attempts to redefine the Mexican family and revise the position of woman in this family. Another Fernández film, *Salón México*, his first set in a contemporary social context, blends elements of realism and melodrama with his particular lyrical style in order to fashion a mythical Mexico wherein female sacrifices are repaid with spiritual, if not social, rewards.

Chapter 5 offers an analysis of the Mexican femme fatale, *la devoradora*. I analyze how the (false) categorization of woman as either virgin or whore escapes narrative containment in Fernando de Fuentes' *Doña Bárbara* and Luis Buñuel's *Susana*. *Doña Bárbara* reveals how the ambiguity of sexual difference is foregrounded through the strategy of masquerade, whereas *Susana* is discussed in terms of its parodic deconstruction of the representation of gender in Mexican film. By using the term "parody," I refer to what Marsha Kinder calls "the ulterior motive of satire." For Kinder, these ulterior motives may work as "strategies of resistance" within the cinematic text (1990, 73–74). Buñuel's film appropriates Mexican filmic conventions to offer up a critique of the ideological discourses of gender and gender relations in Mexico in the 1940s. Although this film was made within the commercial system, the intervention of Buñuel, as both outsider and auteur, cannot be ignored. Finally, in my conclusion, I suggest how film critics might profitably theorize the nature and function of representation of woman in national cinemas in general and in Mexican cinema in particular.

Although numerous histories of cinema are written each year, what is especially important for feminism, according to Patrice Petro, is the writing of film history from a perspective that is concerned with notions of gendered identity, the historical nature of representation, and the function of sexual difference in national cinemas.[4] This volume takes up Petro's challenge by examining the representation of woman in the classical Mexican cinema within the context of Mexican culture in the 1940s.

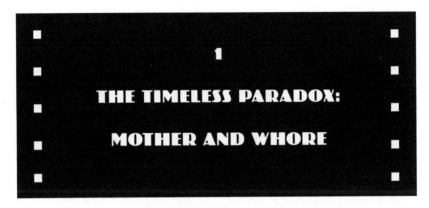

Todas las mujeres son unas putas, menos mi madre, que es una santa.
(All women are whores, except my mother, who is a saint.)
Francisco Sánchez

One of Mexican cinema's earliest sound films, *Santa* (*Saint,* Antonio Moreno, 1931), based on a novel by Federico Gamboa, presents the melodramatic story of a young country girl (Lupita Tovar), conveniently named Santa, who is seduced and then abandoned by a handsome soldier. Banished from the family house in rural Mexico by her angry brothers, Santa is forced to seek refuge in one of the many brothels in Mexico City. Because of her beauty, she becomes a much sought-after prostitute, winning the love of many men, including Jarameno, a famous bullfighter, and Hipólito, a blind piano player who works in the brothel. However, Santa's glory is short-lived. Abandoned by Jarameno, she eventually dies from the effects of poverty, alcoholism, and some unnamed disease, most probably syphilis. In a reading of *Santa* as a specifically Mexican film, Santa has to die, because she cannot be both virgin and whore.

The polarity of bad woman/good woman is of course not unique to Mexico or Mexican cinema. Marina Warner suggests, in fact, that "there is no place in the conceptual architecture of Christian society for a single woman who is neither a virgin nor a whore" (1985, 235). Like women in most cultures, Mexican women have repeatedly been defined by these overdetermined and conflicted constructions of femininity. Hollywood and other national cinemas have appropriated the

Figure 1.1. One of the Mexican cinema's first prostitutes, Santa (Lupita Tovar), symbolizes the Virgin/La Malinche archetypal duality, which Roger Bartra calls the "essential image of the modern Mexican woman." *Santa*, production still.

paradigmatic mother/whore dichotomy by, for instance, situating the virtuous, self-sacrificing mother in opposition to the fallen woman as emblematic representations of womanhood.

However, in the case of Mexican cinema these binary symbols of woman are tied to specific mythohistorical figures: the Virgin of Guadalupe, Mexico's patron saint, who represents the ambiguous figure of the maternal virgin, and La Malinche, the so-called traitor of Mexico. Roger Bartra argues that these two "primordial" archetypes are at the root of the Mexican spirit and form the "essential image of the modern Mexican woman" (1992, 147–150). The Virgin of Guadalupe and La Malinche may thus be seen as archetypes that served as "ready-made" symbols of woman's sexuality and that reappear in various forms throughout Mexican history in literature, drama, and popular culture.[1]

In order to understand the particular representations of woman in Mexican cinema more fully, I want to look at the historical development of the above two figures, who served as archetypes for Mexico's own metanarrative of the virgin/whore polarity. My intent in this chapter is to describe and locate these representations in Mexican myth and history in light of the social context in which they were produced. I will not trace a continuity in the development of the narratives of La Malinche or the Virgin of Guadalupe, but instead will examine their changing historical and mythological significance, with the intention of teasing out what Fredric Jameson calls the "range of meanings" associated with powerful cultural symbols.

Woman as Archetype: Myth and Cultural Narratives

Sandra Messinger Cypess, in her study of La Malinche in Mexican literature, points out that in most Mexican cultural narratives, woman is depicted as a positive but submissive figure, a commodity to be traded among men as mistress, wife, daughter, or servant, as well as an active but destructive, negative figure: the temptress, *la devoradora*, the devourer of men. These attributes, assigned to the Virgin of Guadalupe and La Malinche, have been continually transformed in an attempt to account for the conflicted and changing positions of woman in Mexican psychic and social structures. While the social position of women has been defined by some form of patriarchy since before the Spanish conquest, Mexican patriarchy has manifested itself in particular ways in response to social pressures. These responses have not been indifferent to historical changes.

Like other forms of patriarchy, Mexican patriarchy may be defined "as a system of male-female . . . inequality linked on one hand with culture, kinship and family organization, and on the other with gender roles and relations." In addition, it "is highly institutionalized within the economy as well" (Chant, 1991, 3). In Mexico, patriarchy is pro-

claimed in language (the phrase *hijo de la chingada* [son of a whore]
is considered to be extremely derogatory), in social practice (there is
not only a practice of but also an acceptance of male promiscuity and
physical violence against women among all classes), and in ideological discourse (through nationalist rhetoric that promulgates ideals of
"populism, national unity, and class harmony" while ignoring socially
sanctioned divisions of gender, class, and ethnicities) (Cockcroft, 1983,
147). While all women in Mexico may be oppressed on the basis
of gender, lower-class and Indian women suffer additional abuse due
to their ethnicity and/or their social status. As Maria Herrera-Sobek
notes, while it can be argued that it is the ideology of patriarchy that
generally "informs and structures the archetypal images [of woman],"
it is "class . . . that tempers their specific representation in Mexican
society" and, I would argue, in Mexican cinema (1990, xviii).

In her study of the Mexican *corrido*, a traditional ballad that was
most often written by and for rural campesino classes, Herrera-Sobek
locates four feminine figures that recur in Mexican social and cultural
myths and narratives: "the Good and the Terrible Mother, the Mother
Goddess, the Lover, and the Soldier" (1990, xviii). While each of these
figures symbolizes in a different form the patriarchal roles constructed
for the woman as both mother and sexual object, each also reveals the
paradoxical nature of the mother/whore construction. For example,
the Good Mother represents the self-sacrificing, spiritual superiority
of woman, the suffering mother of Christ weeping for her lost son.
Through this role "the Mexican woman derives power, prestige, and
status from her femininity and her position as mother and wife." According to Herrera-Sobek, the Good Mother archetype thus works to
challenge the stereotype of the passive, spiritual mother by assuming
a dynamic narrative role in the Mexican family structure. Ultimately,
however, this Good Mother emerges as an "ambiguous image," often
referred to by such derogatory expressions as *chinga tu madre* (fuck your
mother) and *puta madre* (whoring mother) (Herrera-Sobek, 1990, 11–
14). Similarly, the Terrible Mother operates as a force that threatens,
causes harm to or interferes with the goal of the hero. Though represented as negative, aggressive, and destructive, at the same time the
Terrible Mother emerges as a dynamic and powerful figure.

Carl Jung theorized the mythic quality of archetypes in order to account for what he found to be repeated "inherited predispositions to apperceive typical or nearly universal situations and figures" in human psyches (Maduro and Wheelwright, 1992, 182). Feminists have criticized Jung's findings primarily for what they consider a disregard of the historical specificity of the representation, the gender, and the function of an archetype. However, Jungian analysts Renaldo J. Maduro and Joseph B. Wheelwright emphasize that Jung never suggested that the specific representation or content of an archetype was inherited. Instead, according to these authors, Jung allowed for the sociohistorical construction. He proposed that two distinct elements define the archetype: It is first of all a "psychoid" or "transcendent" factor in the unconscious that is "built into the structure of the human psychic system." Second, the archetype manifests as an "archetypal image" evoked by cultural and environmental factors (Maduro and Wheelwright, 1992, 181–184). According to this understanding of archetype, notions of male and female, while common to all human cultures, must be understood to be constructed and activated in "culturally patterned ways" (Maduro and Wheelwright, 1992, 186).

Literary critics such as Herrera-Sobek and Warner seek to recuperate Jung's paradigm for feminists by considering the archetype as an "image in process" rather than a fixed prototype. Herrera-Sobek, for example, defines archetypal theory as "a type of analysis that views archetypes as recurrent patterns" dependent on "historical, political, and social forces for their formation" (1990, xiii). Moreover, she differentiates the archetype from the stereotype by suggesting that the archetype "depends on a specific context for its realization and its peculiar traits, [while] the stereotype is a solidified image with no specificity or individuality (1990, xviii)."[2]

While the notion of archetype may not fully explain the historical and cultural function of the Virgin/Mother figure, Warner observes that "such a symbol exercises a sway over our unconscious lives" in numerous guises, at countless moments, and in various contexts (1985, xxiv). The task for feminist critics is to locate and explain the manifestation of this double figure within the context of specific moments and contexts.

La Malinche

Early prototypes of La Malinche and the Virgin of Guadalupe can be found in Mesoamerican legends. For example, two pre-Columbian Mexica (Aztec) female figures, Cihuacóatl and Coyolxauhqui, symbolized a fusion of the Earth Mother and the war goddess. Elizabeth Salas suggests that these figures of feminine power "emerged from the political, economic and social structure of many early Meso-American tribes, wherein some powers related to inheritance, property, and tribal defense passed from mother to daughter" (1990, 2). In Aztec legend, the goddess Coatlícue is depicted as a female deity who "devours all." Chicomecóatl was offered human sacrifices in exchange for personal and community favors. Other goddesses include Itzpapalótl and Mictlanciuatle, both goddesses of death, and Tlazolteotl, the "devourer of wastes," who symbolized sexual excess. Mayan female archetypes included Ixcel, who signified darkness, and other goddesses known for their Amazonlike powers.

Salas goes on to relate that by the sixteenth century, as a more patriarchal and militaristic social order developed, this twin figure was transformed into a "warlike manifestation . . . blood drip[ping] from her shark-toothed mouth" in order to "sever the people from the Earth Mother/war Goddess cult." Later, this ferocious female deity is depicted as a "Snake woman . . . who brought men misery. . . . By night she walked weeping and wailing, a dread phantom foreboding war" (1990, 5–6). In more recent Mexican and Mexican-American legends, the Weeping Woman reappears as La Llorona, who, falsely accused of murdering her children, returns to earth seeking revenge against all men.

What is most interesting about Salas' analysis is that it chronicles these changes in the representation of female goddesses as being aligned with an expanding patriarchy in Mexica society that demanded the annihilation of the goddesses' earlier reputations. As Mexican tribes became more involved with military endeavors, women were relegated to supportive sexual and procreative functions while the men saved their strength for battle.

When the Spanish conquerors arrived in Mexico in the early sixteenth century, they appropriated Mexica and other Indian women as servants to cook, clean, and provide sexual services for their armies as they marched across Mesoamerica. The most famous of these women was Malinalli—or La Malinche, as she became known in Spanish—a non-Mexica Indian woman sold to the Spanish by her own people who eventually become Cortés' mistress and his interpreter.

It is difficult to locate the historical figure of La Malinche accurately because her character has been continually revised in the narratives of Mexican myths and history. Scholars have established that her original Nahautl name was Malinalli and that she was born in the province of Coatzacualco, but conflicting stories explain how she came to be one of the slave girls presented to Cortés on the eve of the Spanish conquest at Tabasco in 1519. Regardless of the "real" historical circumstances, it was recorded in various diaries and early Spanish and Aztec histories that a young woman named Malinalli was one of the slave girls presented to Cortés and that eventually she became his mistress.[3]

The figure of La Malinche remains blurred between the borders of history and of myth; moreover, the relation between the historical figure and the mythical character has shifted over time. Claude Lévi-Strauss suggested that "what gives the myth an operational value is that . . . it explains the present and the past as well as the future" (1958, 209). Myths may be seen as a method of linking discrete events, individual human experiences, and cultural values and beliefs, and of mediating a historical continuum that serves to explain the unexplainable. If, as Lévi-Strauss further argues, the intention of myth in all its repetitious manifestations is to limit internal discrepancies through its mediating function, then we may investigate the recurrence of particular mythical symbols in a culture as an attempt to resolve contradictions within socially constructed patterns of difference.

Because legend suggests that she willingly offered herself to Cortés, La Malinche is usually represented as the woman who betrayed Mexico. The paradigm of the La Malinche legend, according to Sandra Messinger Cypess, reappears throughout history, working to situate women in Mexico as "the root of all trouble, despite their real lack of power in patriarchal society" (1991, 156). La Malinche thus functions as Mexico's own Eve, Christian history's first mother/whore symbol and man's first Other. Although seemingly produced by God to ensure the reproduction of the race, Eve was also the symbol of man's expulsion from paradise and the advent of human death.[4] While Mexico "inherited" the European Christian conception of all women being singularly responsible for "man's" exile, La Malinche, who is remembered as both Mexico's first Mother and the betrayer of Mexico, provided a specifically local manifestation for the discourse of patriarchal nationalism.

Salas argues that by subsequently focusing on the legend of La Malinche as traitor, historians shifted the blame for the destruction of the indigenous peoples from the shoulders of the two males associated with the Spanish conquest, Cortés and Montezuma. Moreover, this myth ignores the central historical consequence of the conquest: the transposition of power from one patriarchal colonial state to another. Previous historical, mythological, and literary analyses of La Malinche have mostly ignored this argument. However, Tzvetan Todorov, in *The Conquest of America*, locates La Malinche as "the second essential figure in this conquest of information," underscoring her role as translator not only of words but also of intentions. In regard to her sexual relationship to Cortés, Todorov "assume[s] that this relationship has a strategic and military explanation rather than an emotional one." He points out how in the *Florentine Codex* (the Aztec account of the first meeting between Cortés and Montezuma), La Malinche "dominates" the illustrations. However, Todorov finally reduces her to merely a "symbol, of the cross-breeding of cultures." Although he does assign La Malinche a more assertive role than conventional history does, Todorov ends up relegating woman to the traditional feminized role of receptacle (1984, 100–101).

Chicana feminist scholars have recently undertaken to revise these early analyses of La Malinche, pointing out, for example, what male historians have generally overlooked: that she was *forced* to assume the role of mistress and interpreter to protect her own life and that of her son.[5] Such revisions will no doubt contribute to new narratives and representations of women in Mexico. My interest here, however, is to examine how and why La Malinche has been used to symbolize the *mala mujer* and the traitor in Mexican history and cultural narratives.

Cypess sees La Malinche as a "literary sign" with multiple meanings, arguing that within various historical contexts, the mythohistorical figure of La Malinche takes on a different significance. Cypess looks primarily at literary representations of La Malinche in texts that are situated in the historical moment of the Spanish conquest, but she also suggests that "the extent to which La Malinche has become part of the Mexican consciousness can be verified further in the number of works that have no ostensible relation to the historical period of the Conquest, yet use the paradigm as a subtext" (1991, 153). In Mexico, the originating scenario that gave birth to constructed social relations among men and women is rooted in the historical significance of the connection among the Spanish conqueror, Cortés; the Indian woman, La Malinche; and the Aztec ruler, Montezuma.

Many scholars have tied this scenario directly to the problem of Mexican identity. Octavio Paz, for example, has theorized that if the mother is *la chingada,* the whore, then Mexicans are by definition *hijos de la chingada,* sons of the violated Mother. If La Malinche is the mother of Mexico, who is the father—the Spanish conqueror, Cortés, or the conquered Indian, Montezuma? Either way, according to Paz, the Mexican people are the product of "violation, abduction or deceit." He writes that this conflicted question of origins "is the central secret of our anxiety and anguish" (1985, 79–81).

However, other critics (most recently, Roger Bartra) have argued that this "central secret" of Malinche's betrayal is merely a continuation of an older myth of Mexican national identity. For Bartra, "what is interesting to emphasize here is the way in which the formulation of the Black Legend of the Malinche is directly related to establishment of the idea of nationhood." This idea did not exist before the arrival of the Spanish, nor did it flourish for a long time afterward. However, with independence from Europe in the nineteenth century came the need to invent a myth of origination, a fatherland, and a family of founding "heroes and traitors" (1992, 155–156).

Virgin of Guadalupe

Bartra contends that "the history of the cult of the Virgin of Guadalupe reflects the evolution of Mexican attitudes towards the female sex" (1992, 154). It is this "history of attitudes" that I want to explore in the following discussion of Mexico's own Indian Virgin.

According to legend, a dark-skinned apparition of the Virgin Mary appeared to an Indian named Juan Diego in 1531, just ten years after the Spanish destruction of the Aztec city of Tenochtitlán. The vision occurred on a hill that had been the site of a temple dedicated to the Aztec virgin Tonantzin, a goddess of corn who was often depicted carrying her divine son in a cradle on her back. Although the Catholic Church officially recognized Juan Diego's vision and allowed a small shrine to be built on Tonantzin's hill, the cult of the Virgin of Guadalupe, as this dark-skinned Mary came to be known, was not immediately sanctioned. Not until a century after Juan Diego's vision, when a Spanish bishop initiated a program to bring the straying Indians back into the fold of the Church, was the Virgin of Guadalupe officially established as Mexico's own Indian Virgin. The cult of this Mother Goddess archetype thus "had its beginnings in a general climate of religious distrust and religious heterogeneity and syncretism" (Herrera-Sobek, 1990, 37).

This incorporation of Guadalupe was materially marked by what Jacques Lafaye describes as "the construction of ever larger and more sumptuous basilicas, three being built in a century and a half." According to Lafaye, the *criollos* (those of Spanish descent born in Mexico) "wanted to make clear that the cult of Guadalupe was the property of [the criollos] implicitly distinguished from the *gachupines* [Spaniards]" (1976, 275).[6]

Cypess defines this syncretic figure as a type of palimpsest, a tablet that has been written on repeatedly but still reveals the marks of previous writing. According to Cypess, the palimpsest is a repeated "architectural structure" in Mexican history: "the [way] Amerindian tribes built one pyramid atop another or how the Catholic church constructed its religious sites in the same places used by indigenous tribes. It also describes the way one group takes advantage of the cultural meanings formed by previous groups, adding, altering, but not completely destroying the previous suppositions" (1991, 171). By building the symbol of the Virgin of Guadalupe upon the existing structure of Tonantzin—both literally and figuratively—indigenous groups were able to incorporate the idea of a Christian universe into an existing religious discourse. However, it also appears that by seemingly allowing the Indians to construct their own meaning of the Virgin, the Catholic Church was more easily able to achieve its larger colonial intent. The story of the Virgin of Guadalupe may thus be seen as part of an attempt to Indianize Catholicism in order to make it more palatable to Indians who were still resistant to Spain's religious proselytizing.

The colonization of Mexico was forged by a very powerful state-church alliance achieved, in part, because the indigenous populations were persuaded to incorporate into their culture certain "meanings" presented to them by the Catholic Church. As suggested above, the development of the particular form of Mexican Catholicism was a merging of indigenous religious practices with the new Christian religion, personified in the figure of the Virgin of Guadalupe.

This cult of Guadalupe ushered in a new phase of Mexican consciousness, framing Mexicanism in what Henry C. Schmidt describes as "a relationship to the non-Hispanic world and pre-Colombian paganism." This relationship was forged through a "broader acceptance of the Indian past and by positing the apostolic origins of Aztec religion and the divine intervention of God" (1978, 15). According to Schmidt, the original creation myth of the birth of Mexico, wherein La Malinche played the part of Eve and Cortés the part of Adam, could now be rewritten. The shame of spiritual and political rape was swept under the carpet of a "pure" Indian heritage and a Virgin birth. This Indian Virgin became the intermediary between the known past and the unknown future, a symbol constructed in an attempt to resolve social and historical contradictions. As Bartra puts it, Guadalupe was used to "create a secular parallel to the Catholic cult" expressly for the purposes of shoring up a fledgling nationalism. It was for this end that she was transformed from a criolla into an Indian: "a maternal virgin and a woman of Babylon. She represents the indigenous past, subjugated and docile, but no one knows what idolatrous lusts lurk deep down" (Bartra, 1992, 156-158).

Other instances of the use of a reinterpreted Virgin Mary figure can be seen in Mexican history. During the Wars of Independence between Spain and Mexico in the nineteenth century (1810-1821), for example, while the Spanish battalions invoked the name of the Virgin de Los Remedios, who was of Spanish origin, Mexican soldiers carried the banner of the Virgin of Guadalupe, calling her María Insurgentes; and during the Wars of the Reform (1858-1861), the Mexicans again raised the banner of the Mexican Virgin of Guadalupe.

The Postindependence Period

The late colonial period in Mexico can be seen as a continuous process of reorganization from a mercantilist-capitalist mode of production to a more purely capitalist one. It was marked by a series of protracted conflicts, including the Wars of Independence (1810–1821) and the Wars of the Reform against the French. After the ultimate defeat of the French in 1867, a liberal-reformist government led by Benito Juárez implemented measures that resulted in the expansion of the economic sectors and the development of a new wage labor proletariat. James Cockcroft notes, however, that the formation of an independent nation-state "by no means put an end to peasant resistance," and the following two decades were marked by continuous social unrest and armed rebellion (1983, 83–84).

After the death of Juárez, a powerful army commander, Porfirio Díaz, seized power in 1876, initiating Mexico's social and political transition to a constitutional dictatorship. Under the prolonged administration of Díaz (1876–1911), most of the material wealth of Mexico was seized by a small upper-class criollo elite in conjunction with foreign investors, primarily from the United States. Between 1898 and 1910, real wages fell and the mortality rate among the lower classes rose. By 1910 most of the members of the indigenous population had lost their communal farmlands to larger domestic and foreign commercial interests (Cockcroft, 1983, 10–11).

Díaz and his supporters rallied behind a philosophy of positivism that promoted the logic of science as the motor of progress. The intent of the *científicos*, as these men were called, was to unify Mexico under a banner of "order and progress." This banner, however, excluded indigenous groups. During Díaz's reign, the Mexican electorate, composed primarily of criollos, was limited to a mere 4 percent of the entire national population.

Under Díaz, Mexico did maintain an unprecedented period of economic growth. However, the more than twenty years of the Porfirian dictatorship also entailed great costs for a new class of disenfranchised rural proletariat. The price of modernization for the majority of the Mexican population included seizures of long-held community land that was subsequently concentrated into larger holdings by wealthy criollo families. This practice contributed to rising unemployment, substandard working conditions, and falling wages as thousands of indigenous peasants were forced off their lands. Frederick Turner describes Díaz's nationalism as merely a "convenient excuse for dictatorship and the maintenance of privilege" (1968, 56).

While the reasons leading up to the Mexican Revolution of 1910 are multiple and complex, the above outline of the social and economic situation that preceded this protracted civil strife provides a historical background for the continued discussion of the representation and position of women in Mexican history. The beginning of the military phase of the Mexican Revolution occurred in 1910. Francisco Madero, leader of the Revolutionary forces, ousted Díaz and took command in 1911, promising the peasant and proletariat classes that the Revolutionary government would implement agrarian and social reforms, a promise on which he later reneged. In response to this failed commitment, General Emiliano Zapata, supported by peasants and workers, issued the Plan de Ayala, a call to continue the struggle until peasant demands were met.

In 1917, conservative forces defeated Zapata and another Indian leader, Pancho Villa, and a civilian government was set up under Venustiano Carranza. This was the beginning of the second or "social" phase of the Mexican Revolution, which introduced policies that, on the surface, directly affected women. President Carranza established a new constitution and, among other reforms, instituted a new law in 1917 regarding familial relations that allowed both men and women to seek and obtain a divorce. In addition, husband and wife were to share authority in family decision-making, and women who were self-sufficient by virtue of inherited money or professional earnings were not obliged to turn their income over to their husbands (Fisher, 1942, 213). However, political affirmation did not translate into day-to-day practice, and traditional relations of male/female power remained virtually unchanged, especially in the home. Lillian Estelle Fisher, writing about the status of Mexican women during the early years of the Revolution, argues that even if "the legal status of man and woman has been equal" since 1917, women have been discouraged from availing themselves of legal protection due to the influence of the Catholic Church and the continuity of patriarchal forms of familial and social structures (1942, 213).

As a number of writers have noted, women were actively involved in the Revolution as *soldaderas* (female soldiers).[7] Although they worked as cooks and nurses, and many carried and used weapons, the *soldaderas* earned praise for sacrificing their bodies to the Revolution—not for laying down their lives but for offering their sexual and procreative abilities to the male revolutionary heroes. In a conservative patriarchal society that placed a high price on a woman's virginity, this was one way of justifying the loss of womanly purity. Ilene O'Malley quotes the poem "La Soldadera," by the Mexican poet Baltasar Dromundo, in which Dromundo "blesses" revolutionary women for opening their "sanctified brown flesh . . . at the command of Emiliano Zapata" (1986, 134–135).

Notwithstanding the Mexican woman's sacrifice, however, the Revolution failed to account for or provide for a new revolutionary position for woman. Although out of economic necessity women moved into nontraditional roles in the labor sector, social and economic changes brought about by the war did not alter the essential patriarchal structure of Mexican society. Women assumed their new roles within another patriarchal system, "provid[ing] a quick way to restore the population's physical and 'moral' health, to make the most efficient use of their meager economic resources, and to create responsible workers for the rebuilding of the economy" (O'Malley, 1986, 138).

Moreover, this "new" system had to legitimate its power as a specifically revolutionary movement. Part of the state's discursive strategy in the early postrevolutionary phase of the 1920s was to forge a national identity through the diffusion of a nationalist rhetoric into social and cultural discourses—a rhetoric that would appear to incorporate not only women but all of Mexico's ethnically, racially, and economically diverse people.[8]

This perspective was perhaps best articulated by José Vasconcelos in his *La raza cósmica (The Cosmic Race)*, written in 1925. Vasconcelos' thesis exemplifies the continued narrativization of Mexican national identity. He writes of the coming of a new age, which he calls an "aesthetic era," wherein a fusion of races and classes in Latin America would culminate in the creation of a new race. Vasconcelos was one of the first to venerate the mestizo as the quintessential Mexican. However, rather than hailing this identity as a synthesis of the best of both cultures, European and Indian, Vasconcelos promoted the new Mexican race by venerating a European cleansing of the indigenous culture. By the 1920s, light-skinned criollos and mestizos comprised the economically and politically dominant classes; darker-skinned Indians "still occupied the lowest rung of society [and] *mestizo* culture regarded its Indian heritage as a source of shame and its European aspects as superior" (O'Malley: 1986, 118).

Where was woman located in this revolutionary discourse on national identity? The basic thesis of O'Malley's argument is that the notion of a specific revolutionary machismo had a calculated ideological function. According to O'Malley, while this revised form of machismo may have shared the basic ideology and expression of male superiority with other forms of patriarchal practices—aggressive sexual and social behaviors, and wife-beating, for example—what gave it its specific quality was its association with Mexican nationalism and its "officialness, its openly proclaimed status as part of the national identity" (1986, 7). Machismo, in Mexico, came to be identified as the major expression of *lo mexicano*, an authentic "Mexicanness."

Álvaro Obregón succeeded to the presidency in 1920. From 1920 until 1940, Mexico focused on strengthening national "familial" ties by realizing some of the social goals of the Revolution. According to Howard Cline, the Mexican Revolution had come to a standstill by 1933, partly as a result of the development of a worldwide depression and "the growing conservatism of Revolutionary generals who had translated political power into personal wealth" under President Plutarco Elías Calles (1924-1928) and the second term of President Obregón from 1928 to 1932 (Cline, 1963, 150-151). However, when President Lázaro Cárdenas assumed power in 1934, Mexico experienced a revolutionary resurgence that included the reorganization of the official political party, an extension of rural education, the expropriation of the Mexican oil industry from foreign companies, and the nationalization of major industries such as the railways and cinema. Cárdenas also instituted the nationalization and subsequent redistribution of privately held land and strengthened the power of the unions by incorporating the labor sector into the Institutional Revolutionary Party (PRI). Some of these new programs specifically addressed the needs of women and resulted in their greater access to economic benefits.

Feminist movements and women's search for a social position in

Mexico began during the first decade of the twentieth century. While it has been argued that Cárdenas supported women in their struggle for suffrage, he was afraid that if they were given the vote, women, whom he felt were naturally conservative, would align themselves with the Catholic Church and other conservative causes. Mexican women did not receive the right to vote in national elections until 1953.

Cárdenas' support of the peasant and working-class population alienated the powerful middle and upper classes, resulting in the formation in 1939 of the only major oppositional party, the Party of National Action (PAN), a coalition of conservative business and professional interests unhappy with Cárdenas' support of the proletariat. President Manuel Ávila Camacho, responding to the political divisiveness of the Cárdenas administration, attempted to rebuild a national coalition. Mexico's major political party, the PRI, became a more conservative force under Ávila Camacho. Although he continued to support some of the protectionist policies of the previous administration, the ties between private entrepreneurs and the state were strengthened.

In the 1940s, Mexico underwent a period of rapid economic transformation in numerous sectors of the economy. With the end of World War II, Mexico and the United States became increasingly interdependent, with the United States expanding its investments in Mexico and bringing new technologies and modes of industrial and agricultural production into the country. This situation, combined with President Ávila Camacho's shift from the socialist policies of Cárdenas' administration toward a more capitalist-based economy, contributed to an unprecedented political and economic stability. Cockcroft writes that between 1940 and 1960, "a 120 percent jump in industrial production and a 100 percent increase in agricultural output" occurred (1983, 150).

In addition, because production became centralized in urban factories and large farms, there was an unprecedented migration of low-skilled and unskilled labor from isolated rural areas into Mexico City and other urban centers (Cockcroft, 1983, 151). A new proletariat emerged to fuel this industrialization process that subsequently required revised notions of gendered social positions.

The Revolution and the continuing growth of industrialization and urbanization led to changes in the Mexican family, bringing women out of the home and church, where they had remained isolated from political concerns. As noted previously, postrevolutionary Mexican women occupied multiple and conflicting social spaces. Some had been *soldaderas*, the women who accompanied their men to war, while others worked as teachers and lawyers and even held public offices.

The problem for postrevolutionary discourse was to construct a female identity that would encompass the myth of the Revolution, which promised social equality; support women entering the workforce; and still fall within the defining borders of patriarchy, which demanded the perpetuation of inequality and socially sanctioned forms of sexual subjugation. After the Revolution, women were expected to take up their old roles of whore and virgin in the spaces assigned to them (the brothel, the church, or, most important, the home). Yet in an increasingly industrial society that required a larger labor force, a space was also made available to women in the workplace. Turner points out that in Mexico, "once women assumed the new jobs, they remained in them, as it became clear that technology permitted and encouraged their participation" (1968, 183).

While Turner's point about women remaining in the economic sector is important, the reasons for this shift were grounded in larger concerns than technological change. An unprecedented economic boom, stepped-up industrialization, and the reinstitution of the bracero program with the United States, in which thousands of Mexican men contracted with the United States for temporary work, combined to pressure women to continue working outside the home. This alteration in women's economic roles threatened existing traditional structures, including the family and patriarchy, which in turn threatened male identity. While women in Mexican society were gaining more social, economic, and political power, Mexican males were dealing with a sense of dislocation in relation to their traditional patriarchal function as the prime movers of culture.

Before 1930, women's position in Mexican society had been narrowly circumscribed by the family, the Church, and sexual function. However, in an era of rapid industrialization, women had to be addressed as members of the workforce and as consumers. Thus, a new definition of woman was needed to legitimate modern social structures and relations of power. This definition had to somehow incorporate revised symbols of nationalism into existing representations of gender.

Mexican cinema became one site wherein this struggle was waged and new symbols of the Mexican woman were shaped.

Myth and Reality

According to Bartra, "the complex myth about the Mexican woman" had begun to be codified after the Wars of Independence in the nineteenth century. He describes the "double-headed *la Chingadalupe*" created by the national culture for the Mexican male "so he will have a partner in his expulsion from Eden. . . . She is both tender and violated, a protectress and a bawd, sweet and treacherous, a maternal virgin and a woman of Babylon. She represents the indigenous past, subjugated and docile, but no one knows what idolatrous lusts lurk deep down" (1992, 158).

Images of La Malinche and the Virgin of Guadalupe were again revised and reincorporated into the social and cultural narratives of the Mexican Revolution. As noted above, in the 1930s and 1940s, the narratives of Mexican gendered identity were threatened by historical forces that jeopardized sanctioned ideas regarding social positions based on gender, relations between men and women, and the stability of what Jean Franco terms "the holy family of the post-revolutionary state." In this modern family, women were required to "accede voluntarily to their own subordination not to a biological father but to a paternal state," which emerged in place of the original ethnic and regional family destroyed by the violence of the Revolution. Through processes of ideological and discursive assimilation, Franco argues, women (as well as Indians and the lower mestizo classes) were incorporated into the "mythic family of the nation" (1989, 148). It will be seen, for example, that in Fernández's film *Río Escondido*, the schoolteacher heroine, Rosaura, is personally sent by President Miguel Alemán to participate in the incorporation of disenfranchised rural Indians into the new Mexican nation.

Outside the home, while an attempt was made to assimilate women into the new postrevolutionary secular state, women were maintaining their positions as the "mortal female body that sustains the male hero" (O'Malley, 1986, xx). In this way, revolutionary and cultural practices were gendered, liberating males—at least in theory—while continuing to oppress females. Thus the state's reinforcement of the ideology of machismo conveniently inserted women into the marketplace as wage labor while keeping them "in their place." Franco notes that the Revolution, in an attempt to shore up disenfranchised males, "constituted a discourse that associated virility with social transformation in a way that marginalized women at the very moment when they were, supposedly, liberated" (1989, 102).

One of the further consequences of the Revolution was that lower-class men, though still denied fundamental economic and social benefits, could now participate in privileges previously refused them, such as the continued subjugation of women. However, "although women shared in the improved status of their classes," under patriarchy they were still oppressed as women (O'Malley, 1986, 136).

If the era of Cárdenas can be measured as a social "boom," the 1940s is seen as the decade of an economic boom in which the country, under the leadership of Ávila Camacho (1940-1946) and Miguel Alemán (1946-1952), experienced unprecedented economic growth. Whereas in 1910 less than 4 percent of women in Mexico had been considered economically active, by 1930 women constituted about 6.9 percent (approximately 372,000) of the total national labor force; "since 1930, women have been entering the work force [in Mexico] at a more rapid rate than the men." Between 1940 and 1950 the percentage of women in the Mexican labor force doubled to approximately 13 percent. These figures do not include the unrecorded numbers of women employed at home on a piece rate basis, making commodities such as clothing and shoes (Singer, 1969, 85-86).[9]

Although the postrevolutionary economic boom did allow economic mobility for Mexican women, the Revolution did not change the essentially patriarchal structure of Mexican social relations. As the Spanish conquest marked a shift from one form of patriarchy to another, so too did the Mexican Revolution signal a similar reorganization.

Paz, in *The Labyrinth of Solitude*, provides one of the most visual descriptions of this reorganization of Mexican machismo, writing that the new Mexican macho "represents the masculine pole of life." He is the *gran chingón*, the aggressor. According to Paz, "one word sums up the aggressiveness, insensitivity, invulnerability, and other attributes of macho: power" (1985, 80–81). Paz further suggests that the model for this figure of power is the Spanish conquistador, the ultimate father of modern Mexicans, who achieved his power through aggressiveness, rape, and destruction.

Writing more than thirty years after Vasconcelos, Paz extends Mexico's "philosophical" search for a national identity. Unlike most writers before him, however, Paz attempts (though unsuccessfully) to place the Mexican woman within the borders of this identity. In his essay, Paz describes the position of woman in Mexican society as one constructed through the intersection of the social discourses of history and popular culture. Paz suggests that a parallel exists between the historical figure of La Malinche, *la chingada*, and the way in which Mexican men relate to women as the "other," writing that "in a world made in man's image, woman is only a reflection of masculine will and desire. When passive, she becomes a goddess, a beloved one, a being who embodies the ancient, stable elements of the universe: the earth, motherhood, virginity" (1985, 36). Though Paz may have perceptively described the actual ideological position of woman in Mexican cultural thought, he has been rightly criticized for failing to acknowledge its inaccurate foundation and thus perpetuating this patriarchal narrative.

The Labyrinth of Solitude was Paz's analysis of the collective Mexican psyche, written at a time when Mexico was experiencing unprecedented economic growth and political stability. However, like Vasconcelos and Samuel Ramos before him, Paz produced an analysis informed by a Mexican middle-class preoccupation with the question of national identity and by a refusal (or inability) to deal with historical and material forces of history.

Analyzing the postrevolutionary Mexican national character as being defined by an inferiority complex, Paz further suggests that in an attempt to compensate for an unsatisfactory male identity forged through conquest and colonization, the Mexican male put on a mask of machismo. Arguing that the "Spanish-Arabic inheritance is only a partial explanation" of Mexican machismo, Paz instead blames machismo partly on woman. Looking to pre-Columbian religious influences that linked woman with nature, Paz finds what he calls a "cosmic analogy." According to Paz, woman's "hidden, passive sexuality" is like a "secret and immobile sun" around which men circulate (1985, 37–38).

Although Paz acknowledges the "falsity of this conception," he insists it is the basis for the Mexican male's relation to women. In doing so, he devalues the historical significance of the Spanish conquest while also dismissing other expressions of Mexican machismo related to class and ethnicity. For Paz, Mexican history is merely the "effect" of Mexican identity that "helps us to understand certain traits of our character" (1985, 73).

Conversely, critics such as Monsiváis and O'Malley argue that rather than being a psychological crutch or philosophical construct, modern Mexican machismo is actually part of a larger revolutionary discourse of national identity that produced a myth about the intention and effects of the Revolution in order to "[co-opt] the revolutionary potential of the popular classes" (O'Malley, 1986, 7). O'Malley contends that the infusion of popular discourses with the "values and psychology of patriarchy" worked to disguise the fact that the Revolution had not succeeded in restructuring the social and material relationships of the Mexican classes that denied lower-class and indigenous men their manhood in the first place.

Machismo functioned on two levels in Mexico in the postrevolutionary period. First of all, there was the more obvious level defining male and female relations. O'Malley also points to a paternal level wherein the state exerted its (political and social) control over subjugated classes as a father would over his son (1986, 140). A similar kind of pseudofamilial relation had existed before the Revolution, in the eighteenth and nineteenth centuries, between the hacienda owner and his workers. Eric Wolf analyzed this social relation and found that "the hacienda bound men not only through debts or through force but also through ties of love and hate" (1959, 208).

Finally, it was possible to institutionalize the ideology of machismo in postrevolutionary discourse precisely because it did not challenge the real socioeconomic basis of power. Because patriarchal values of male superiority were already embedded in traditional Mexican culture, new forms of machismo were readily assimilated into postrevolutionary discourse.

I have argued that the 1930s and 1940s formed a period in Mexican history in which the social positions of women were being redefined within discourses of nationalism, which described the relations be-

tween the state and its subjects, and machismo, which redefined gendered identities. Women were oppressed in new ways, and these new
oppressions emerged out of revised notions of gender, generating new
forms of representations in Mexican cinema and other cultural forms.

As I will show in the next chapter, the figure of woman in Mexican
cinema in the 1940s emerged as a location of an uncertain struggle to
redefine national identity in the shift from the reformist era of Cárdenas to the more conservative administrations of Ávila Camacho and
Alemán. During this period, women were still required to function as
idealized virgin and sexually alluring whore; the virgin worked to shore
up nationalism and the family, the whore to support patriarchy and the
myth of Mexican male identity. Both were incorporated into narratives
of national identity. Mexican cinema revealed these contradictions in
its representations of this "new" woman and in the various positions
she occupied in film narratives. As Francisco Sánchez notes, the portrayal of woman in the classical Mexican film melodrama constantly
"oscillates between these two poles" of virgin and whore (1989, 12).

2

MEXICAN CINEMA AND

THE WOMAN QUESTION

In December 1895, the Lumière brothers presented the first public film exhibition. In April 1896, Edison conducted the first U.S. screening, in New York City. Only a few months later, the Lumières introduced their invention to Mexico City, Rio de Janeiro, and Buenos Aires. Within a few years, a number of Latin American countries, including Mexico, were engaged in their own film production.

Alejandro Galindo explains the limits of production during the silent era of Mexican film, arguing that Mexico was too preoccupied with convulsive political, social, and economic revolutions to concentrate on the development of a cinema of fiction (1985, 25–26). Although there was some film production in Mexico these early years, all equipment and film stock were imported from France and the United States, as were the majority of films, though local firms handled distribution (Schnitman, 1984, 16).[1] The bulk of early Mexican films were newsreels and documentaries about local, regional, and national events.

However, Emilio García Riera points out that despite social instability, and the lack of money, equipment, and studios, Mexican filmmakers did manage to produce a significant number of silent fiction films. Salvador Toscano Barragan released *Don Juan Tenorio* in 1899; the Alva brothers produced *El Grito de Dolores* (*The Shout of Dolores*, 1908), *El súplico de Cuauhtémoc* (*The Torture of Cuauhtémoc*, 1910), and *La banda del automóvil gris* (*The Gray Car Gang*, 1919, with Enrique Rosas); and Mimí Derba's Azteca Films released *En defensa propia* (*In Self-Defense*) in

1917 (Mora, 1989, 11–14). One of the most prolific early film producers, Miguel Contreras Torres, produced and directed eight films between 1919 and 1927 (García Riera, 1969, I, 10). In all, Mexico generated over a hundred silent features and documentaries between 1898 and 1930.[2]

Although Mexico's first full-length feature film, *1810 o los libertadores de México* (Manuel Cirerol Sanores, 1916), was about the 1812 War of Independence, French films such as *Les miserables* (1912) and *Camille* (1912) were the most popular films with Mexican audiences until 1914, when World War I interfered with European film production and Hollywood began to dominate Mexico's screens. By 1928, 90 percent of all films exhibited throughout Mexico and Latin America were produced in the United States (Schnitman, 1984, 16–17). In addition, Hollywood companies controlled the distribution market, in part as a result of the support of the U.S. government, which established the Motion Picture Section in the Bureau of Foreign and Domestic Commerce.[3]

Hollywood's monopoly was eventually challenged, with the widespread introduction of sound films in the 1930s. The shift from silent to sound films required huge capital investments for both production and exhibition; it also created language barriers that helped bolster national film industries in Latin American countries such as Mexico and Brazil. Hollywood studios attempted to counter the threat of domestic production and maintain their economic control through the production of Spanish-language versions of certain films. However, Latin American audiences rejected both Hollywood's "Spanish" sound films, with their mixture of Latin American and Andalusian accents, and subtitled films, which were incomprehensible to the millions of people who were illiterate. Unexpectedly, sound thus opened the way for a national Mexican cinema with Mexican stories, dialects, and songs.

In addition to the language problem, the worldwide economic depression of the 1930s created an impetus for increased industrialization in Latin America. Deprived of easy access to previously imported consumer goods, Latin American countries moved toward greater economic self-sufficiency. In Mexico, this was evident in the growth of a number of industries, including cinema. In the 1930s, film became a centralized and nationalized industry when President Cárdenas established a protectionist policy that included tax exemptions for film productions; the creation of Financiadora de Películas, a state institution mandated to find financing for films; and a system of loans for the establishment of major film studios. In 1932 only six films were produced in Mexico; only one year later, twenty-one films were released. In 1938, Mexican studios produced fifty-seven films (García Riera, 1963, 25).

Much of this success, due to state intervention, came at a price: many smaller producers were forced out of the market. President Ávila Camacho was instrumental in creating the Film Bank, a private institution that helped to combine some of the larger production and distribution companies into one large, integrated firm. At the same time, the state-controlled Banco Cinematográfico made loans only to selected private producers. These kinds of centrist policies contributed to the consolidation of large studios at the expense of smaller producers. However, supported by state protectionist policies, private capital, and U.S. interests located in Mexico, Mexican domestic production was able to increase from forty-one films in 1941 to seventy films in 1943. More important, Mexico's share of its domestic market grew from 6.2 percent in 1941 to 18.4 percent in 1945 (King, 1990, 53).

As World War II spread across Europe, closing major markets for Hollywood films, overseas revenues of the U.S. film industry fell sharply.[4] Hollywood turned to Latin America and began to intensify its penetration of those markets. In 1940, President Franklin Roosevelt created the Office of the Coordinator of Inter-American Affairs (CIAA) with the intention of promoting his "Good Neighbor Policy" in Latin America. Believing that U.S. films could play an important role in the promotion of relations with the southern hemisphere, Roosevelt established a Motion Picture Division within the CIAA. Mexico and other Latin American countries responded by implementing new protective tariffs and import/export controls, and strengthening existing protectionist policies. President Miguel Alemán continued to encourage governmental support of Mexican film by abolishing income taxes for the domestic film industry.

However, the vitality of a national cinema cannot be evaluated solely on the basis of numbers and statistics. Films, even those produced within an industrial context, are more than commodities; they are revelations of cultural meaning, windows onto what Fredric Jameson calls the "political unconscious" of particular historical moments.

In order to understand a cinema as "national," it is important to examine the stylistic, thematic, and generic influences that underlie a cinematic practice as well as the social and cultural pressures that gave rise to that particular practice.

The Development of a National Cinema

As I have noted elsewhere, Sergei Eisenstein's visit to Mexico in 1932 and his film *Que viva México!* are often credited with influencing both the style and the content of Mexican classical cinema.[5] However, Eisenstein's interest in Mexican culture was evident long before his visit to Mexico. He read extensively about Mexico for a 1920 theatrical production of Jack London's story "The Mexican." In 1926 he met the Mexican muralist Diego Rivera in Moscow and was thereafter influenced by Rivera and other Mexican muralists (Helpren, 1932, 13–14).[6]

Though not denying that certain stylistic practices and compositional techniques found in later Mexican films were influenced by the stark landscapes, low-angle camera shots, and reverential representations of Indians in *Que viva México!*, Ramirez Berg argues that it is equally important to recognize Mexican filmmakers' debt to their own artistic, theatrical, and cultural histories for thematic and formalistic inspiration, and their attention to Mexican politics and history for their subjects. Mexican art and popular culture also influenced Mexican directors in their search for a basis for a culturally specific Mexican cinema capable of developing its own genres and stories.

The 1920s, 1930s, and 1940s constituted a period in Mexican history when many writers, artists, and intellectuals were intent on developing a cultural nationalism. They embraced various nationalist discourses such as anti-Americanism and *indigenismo*, an ideological glorification of the mythical origins of *lo mexicano*, an "authentic" Mexicanness. Benedict Anderson has demonstrated how the notion of a common national identity is held together by a complex web of "imagined" bonds. These social, cultural, and linguistic bonds function by responding to shared belief systems that structure both public and private life. Through these communal systems, a history is constructed that appears to lead up to a present moment. However, in the case of Mexico, where a tenuous notion of a common national identity was manufactured through a long and conflicted history of conquest, colonization, and civil strife, issues of regional loyalties, language, ethnicity, and gender divide communities from the postrevolutionary "imagined" construction of a Mexican nation.

The postrevolutionary "imagined community" of Mexico was grounded in what Bartra has termed a nostalgic "mythical paradise" of an invented agrarian history that is populated by a "peasant hero" (1992, 17–21). According to Bartra, this mythical history was produced through postrevolutionary discourse, by artistic and intellectual elites who wanted to cast off the remains of European influence in order to reveal what they perceived as an "essential" Mexican culture. Working from similar motivations, Mexican filmmakers searched for ways to transform an industry dominated by Hollywood and European models into a uniquely Mexican cinema. Many of their strategies, borrowed from Mexican art, theater, and literature, were visible in Mexican films by the late 1930s.

Ramirez Berg cites the painters Guadalupe Posada (1852–1913) and Gerardo Murillo (Dr. Atl, 1875–1964) as two of the major influences on the classical Mexican cinematic style (1992b, 28). While a number of Mexican painters who had studied in Europe aligned themselves with an early Mexican avant-garde movement known as the Movimiento Estridentista (the Strident Ones), modeled on the manifestos of European futurists and Dadaists, other painters, most notably Dr. Atl and Posada, fostered what they perceived as a long-ignored connection to Mexico's own cultural and artistic traditions. Intent on identifying themselves with the masses, these artists adapted elements from popular culture, as well as Mayan and Aztec influences, into their work as a political statement about the nature of Mexican national culture.

For example, drawing inspiration for his paintings from stories of real-life grisly crimes and accidental deaths that he culled from daily newspapers, Posada was an important influence on the muralists. According to Sarah M. Lowe, Posada's work provided Mexican artists with a "crucial link between a folk tradition and the Mexican Modernist practice . . . with a model of an art that was inherently Mexican" (1991, 83–84).

Many film directors of the 1930s and 1940s emerged from the well-educated upper classes of Mexican society and had been active in alternative artistic and theatrical endeavors before they turned to cinema. Julio Bracho (1909–1978), for example, who made twenty films over a period of thirty years, began his career in the Mexican theater in the 1930s and was one of the founding members of an experimental theater group, Escolares del Teatro. Another important film director of the 1930s and 1940s, Juan Bustillo Oro, together with Mauricio Magdaleno, started the Teatro de Ahora, dedicated to interrogating Mexico's social and political problems. According to Ruth S. Lamb, the primary purpose of Escolares del Teatro, Teatro de Ahora, and other experimental companies was "to rid the theatre of its outworn traditions and its antiquated styles of acting, directing, and stage design" and to "liquidate the European influence" (1975, 7–11).

In the early 1900s, Mexican theater looked primarily to Europe for its inspiration. Even in cases where Mexican themes were portrayed, traditional theater incorporated the styles of French and Italian comedy of manners and costume melodramas (Lamb, 1975, 7). Many young playwrights and directors, absorbed with developing a more cosmopolitan theatrical practice, translated and introduced the works of European authors such as Ibsen and Pirandello to Mexican audiences. Even while criticizing the commercial theater for its conventionalism and reliance on traditional European models, these writers ignored their own cultural traditions, preferring to experiment with European artistic movements such as surrealism, expressionism, and other avant-garde practices. From 1910 to 1918, the *género chico* (short play), performed in traveling tent shows and later in urban music halls, was the only theatrical form that managed to find a popular audience. This melodramatic short play drew on folkloric and popular themes, according to Lamb, and often was circumscribed with political overtones (1975, 7).[7]

As discussed earlier, the postwar era was one of widespread nationalistic fervor, and many artists and writers turned to Mexican history and political themes for inspiration. Drawing on other popular theatrical forms, such as the Spanish zarzuelas (musical farces) and their own Mexican *géneros chicos* and *revistas* (parodic musicals based on newspaper articles about dramatic events in Mexican social and political life), these young producers and writers rejected operatic spectacle, historical *costumbres* (costume dramas), and highly stylistic experimental forms, in favor of more naturalistic and realistic styles.[8]

García Riera suggests that the Mexican cinema developed mainly as a hybrid of many of the genres of the Mexican theater, incorporating the musical elements of the zarzuelas and the plots of the revistas but lacking their political references (1986, 225). There were four principal cinematic formulas in place by the end of the 1930s: the *comedia ranchera*, a kind of cowboy musical that incorporated elements of comedy, tragedy, music, and folkloric or nationalistic themes; the highly successful comedic farces of Tin Tan and Cantinflas; the historical epic, which, like those of many other national cinemas, concentrated on patriotic narratives; and the family melodrama, which embodied the elements of patriarchal ideology while focusing on traditional themes of home and religion (Mora, 1989, 56–58). As in other national cinemas, the meanings and articulations of the narrative and stylistic systems of the Mexican cinematic genres were grounded in specifically Mexican narrative, representational, and thematic traditions. And, like the genres of the classical Hollywood cinema, those of the Mexican film served specific functions for Mexican audiences.[9]

Melodrama and the Mexican Cinema

These four Mexican genres continued into the 1940s, a decade that also saw the emergence of groups of films that did not fit neatly into these classifications. Many of these films combined earlier generic influences with melodramatic forms, themes, and stylistic excesses.

In Europe, melodrama in its modern form appeared in the nineteenth century in the popular fictions read voraciously by a newly literate urban populace. Early British Victorian novels were concerned with the circumscription of romance and sex within the domestic circle of the emerging middle-class, nuclear family. In France, the rise of the melodramatic novel was associated with political and social shifts brought about by the French Revolution, the rise of the bourgeoisie, and what Peter Brooks describes as the "privatization and 'desocialization' of art" (1976, 82).

Brooks has argued that the emergence of modern forms of melodrama — specifically the novel and popular theater — was tied directly to shifts in moral, social, and political perspectives in Western culture. These shifts were directed away from a sacred explanation of meaning and toward one that was more secular. Brooks sees this move as a collective "response to the loss of tragic vision" (1976, 14–15). This change in epistemology also signaled the rise of a new form of individualized anxiety that contributed to a disruption in "traditional patterns of moral order." According to Brooks, a new code of human behavior needed to be invented, and melodrama partly met this demand (1976, 20).

Melodrama had been dismissed by early film theorists because of its association with low or mass culture and commercialism. Critical examinations of film melodrama emerged at the end of the 1960s, however, when auteur analysis and mise-en-scène criticism fused with ideological analysis. Melodrama, which had previously been denigrated as merely an example of authorial stylistic excess and relegated to the lowly ranks of popular culture as "merely" a woman's genre, came to be examined as a formal and aesthetic strategy that revealed the tensions and contradictions of bourgeois ideology. One consequence of this critical move was that more attention was paid to certain Hollywood films of previously ignored directors, such as Douglas Sirk and Vincent Minnelli, whose stylistic excesses had formerly been examined under the category of aesthetics.

Film melodrama was circumscribed by conventions of plot, character, and narrative structure, as well as by stylistic and aesthetic elements. Theorists further situated melodrama in opposition to Hollywood's "classic realist text," which for some writers represented "literary cultural tradition, bourgeois ideology and the manipulations of the capitalist culture industries," and for others, portrayed the endless repetition of Freud's originating oedipal scenario (Gledhill, 1987, 8). The melodramatic films of Sirk and others were subsequently seen as examples of an aesthetic and formal subversion of both realism and bourgeois ideology rather than simply authorial interventions. Thomas Elsaesser, in an early and influential essay, argued that certain films of Sirk, for instance, were "critical social documents" (1986, 306).

However, as Christine Gledhill points out, this approach failed to account for the appeal of melodrama to audiences divided by "class, gender, race, [and] age" (1987, 11). For instance, although the figure of woman often performs similar narrative functions in the melodramas of many national cinemas, her representations are remade in response to social, political, and economic transformations. In order to be able to explain both its broad appeal and its specific ideological manifestations, melodrama needs to be historically differentiated.

As in Europe, the melodramatic genre in Latin America was acted upon by social, aesthetic, and industrial determinants within globally changing forms of production and consumption. The Latin American scholar Jesús Martín-Barbero has examined the changing role of melodrama in Latin America, recognizing that many of the elements found in older forms of European popular melodrama made their way to Latin America in new forms.

According to Martín-Barbero, Latin American melodrama privileges spectacle over representation, sacrifices complexity for intensity, reduces all oppositional categories to "good versus evil," substitutes gestures for psychology, and narrativizes plots as familial tensions. While this description could apply to the melodramatic mode in general, in the classical Mexican film the *expressions* of these elements are distinctly Mexican and may be tied directly to the problem of Mexican identity and to the conflicts within the Mexican family caught up in the throes of cultural and political crises.

In Mexico, as in other cultures, melodrama has endured as a popular genre through various technological changes, in part because it has served a mediating function between older forms of narrative and the newer forces of modernity. Martín-Barbero suggests that melodrama in Latin America functions as a mediation between existing and emergent cultures in order to address the specific social and cultural needs of changing populations (1993, 119). Melodrama in Mexican popular culture can perhaps be best understood as metaphoric in its attempt to grasp new levels of social relationships through an exploration of complex and changing familial and social relations.

Ana M. López finds that the melodramatic in Mexican cinema "intersects with three master narratives of Mexican society: religion, nationalism, and modernization." According to López, while the classical Mexican film melodrama deals with these narratives, it is defined in addition by three major functions. First, as a "drama of identification," Mexican film melodrama operated as a "symbolic reenactment" of the originating scenario of the formation of Mexican identity—the drama of the Cortés/Malinche/Montezuma triad. Second, López suggests that Mexican melodrama was more "excessive" than Hollywood melodrama, with excess being a form of resistance to Hollywood's dominance. Finally, she writes that the film melodrama in Mexico "served as the principal vehicle for the transmission of new habits and the reiteration of codes of behavior" for the newly urban, poor working class (1991a, 32–36). In other words, it was not merely that Mexicans went to the movies to see themselves as they were; rather, they went to learn how they should "become." These three thematic functions of origination, resistance, and cultural transmission define the cultural specificity of Mexican melodrama.

Certain general features of film melodrama do persist, however, across national boundaries. Two of the most pervasive are melodrama's focus on familial and sexual conflicts. Ramirez Berg argues that the overarching concern in the classical Mexican melodrama was the family, writing that all ideological factors, including "bourgeois values, patriarchy, *machismo*, capitalism, heterosexuality—and solitude" were centered on shoring up this institution that was being challenged by political, economic, and cultural changes initiated during the Mexican Revolution (1992a, 18).

While not denying the centrality of the family in postrevolutionary Mexican discourse, I want to suggest that the emphasis on the family in Mexican films of the 1940s was ultimately grounded in the "woman question." For Mexico, this question evolved around the construction of a revised position for women in a new Mexican society, a construction that proved troubling for a postrevolutionary hegemony as well as for narrative cinema.

The problem of sexual difference is particularly obvious in film melodrama. For example, Gledhill has observed that while the figure of woman in melodrama is often read as the object of male desire, she is also "a generator of female discourses drawn from the social realities of women's lives," offering an explicit resistance to patriarchal discourse (1987, 37). Although the classical Hollywood cinema has been the primary focus of feminist film scholars, feminist critics have recently turned to other national cinemas to explore these complex representations.[10]

In the following chapters, I will show how certain contradictions organized representations of the Mexican woman in the Mexican films of the 1940s. Although Franco claims that Mexican cinema was as "efficient as the classical Hollywood cinema in creating spectator identification and relaying it by means of a narrative plot that mapped the spectator into a process of change," it had a difficult time map-ping women into a new narrative consciousness because they were also called on to fulfill the same roles they had occupied prior to the Revolution (1989, 147).

Judith Mayne locates similar problems in early Soviet films. She argues that the representations of femininity in these silent films work to subvert narrative coherence by introducing an element of ambiguity. She writes that the Soviet films are ambiguous not in the sense of their relation to cinematic conventions of the 1920s but "in the sense that they illuminate the contradictions that are inevitable when the development of an art form, and particularly a nascent art form such as the cinema, is intertwined with an ideological agenda and with social transformation" (1989, 9).

Although it would be difficult to equate Mexico in the 1940s with Soviet Russia in the 1920s, there were a number of comparable relations exhibited between cinema and society in both instances. Like the Soviet cinema of the 1920s, the Mexican cinema was very much bound up with a postrevolutionary agenda for social transformation, an agenda that had been on the table since 1920. And, as in the Soviet films Mayne discusses, the representation of woman in many of the Mexican films of the 1940s was conflicted. This conflict can be traced to social and narrative tensions surrounding cinema, gender, and social transformation in Mexico in the 1940s.

For example, looking at Emilio Fernández's 1947 film *Enamorada*, Franco describes how the film's narrative strategy, attempting to reconcile a new revolutionary ethics with the older, patriarchal structure, is temporarily disrupted by the figure of woman. *Enamorada* is a loosely adapted melodramatic version of Shakespeare's *Taming of the Shrew* — or in Mexican terms, the taming of the masculinized modern woman. The major female protagonist, Beatriz, may be seen as a force mediating two levels of the film by negotiating between the narrative level of the melodramatic text and the social level of ideology. Elizabeth Salas criticizes *Enamorada* for its "lack of realism," and because "the director imposes his own view about women and their roles in the Revolution" (1990, 99). However, as Franco sees it, it is the narrative trajectory, not the director, that works to suppress or resolve gender and class conflicts through strategies of containment that control both the film's structure and its resolution. Franco writes that "the narrative therefore must restore the balance by affirming masculinity and subduing the 'virile' female" (1989, 149).

As will be seen, the figure of woman emerges as a disruptive narrative and representational force in many classical Mexican films of the 1940s. Though I recognize the importance of close textual analysis, my concern is to place these analyses within the context of historical, social, and aesthetic issues surrounding the production of narrative film in Mexico in the 1940s, in order to explore how the notion of woman intersects with those of history and cinema.

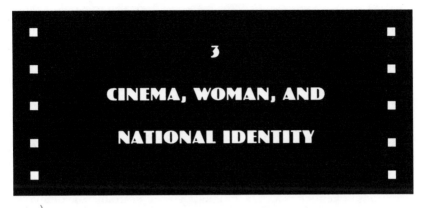

3

CINEMA, WOMAN, AND

NATIONAL IDENTITY

More than any other cultural instrument . . . [the classical
Mexican cinema] reshaped the notion of Mexican
national identity by turning nationalism into a great show.

Carlos Monsiváis

While the relation between national identity and woman has been
explored within the context of a number of national cinemas, some
would ask why the notion of a "female" national identity needs to be
interrogated as a specific condition apart from a history of the formation of national identity in general.[1] As I see it, while women may share
certain historical experiences with men on the basis of class, for example, their experiences *as women* give them a fundamentally different
set of relationships to the "nation," relationships that may be couched
in political or economic rhetoric but that are ultimately grounded in
ideologies of sexual difference. In many instances, the idea of woman
is often collapsed into that of nation, so that the constructed notion
of the "feminine" becomes a powerful representation of the creative
potential of the national.

At the same time, the choice to focus on the peculiar and diverse
relations of woman to nation does not indicate a disregard of other
predicators of national identity. Such a disregard would in itself ignore
the heterogeneity of female national *identities*, which often are modified
by racial, religious, or class divisions.

In Mexico, a number of films of the 1940s explored this relation
between gender and national identity. *Cuando los hijos se van* (Juan Bus-

tillo Oro, 1941), *Virgen de medianoche* (Alejandro Galindo, 1941), *La china poblana* (Fernando A. Palacios, 1943), *Flor Silvestre* (Emilio Fernández, 1943), *La mujer sin alma* (Fernando de Fuentes, 1943), *Las abandonadas* (Emilio Fernández, 1944), *Crepúsculo* (Julio Bracho, 1944), *La devoradora* (Fernando de Fuentes, 1946), and *Enamorada* (Emilio Fernández, 1946) are but a few of the more successful films of this era that sought to mediate the complex articulations of woman and gendered relations.

In this chapter, I will discuss two films directed by Emilio Fernández, who is often referred to as the founder of the Mexican school of filmmaking. In both *María Candelaria* (1943) and *Río Escondido* (1948), questions of gender, class, and ethnicity converge around the drama of Mexican nationalism and female national identity. On the one hand, these films appear to propose new positions for women within the rhetoric of national identity. At the same time, however, they struggle to support nationalist discourses and the national myths of social change.

National Identity and Gender in Mexico: *La madre patria*

The identity of woman and the identity of nation in postrevolutionary Mexico were blurred by the paradoxical concept of *la madre patria*.[2] According to Frederick Turner, who traces the development of Mexican nationalism from the end of the nineteenth century to the 1940s, the constellation of discourses that made up la madre patria represented an attempt to forge a national solidarity among the diverse elements of the Mexican population despite differences of language, ethnic and cultural traditions, class, race, gender, and regional affiliation. By privileging a common (if invented) history, the Spanish language, a national system of education, and the mestizo as the quintessential Mexican, la madre patria came to signify a unified Mexican nation. At the same time, social and political divisions were maintained along class, race, and gender lines through the legitimation of two specific postrevolutionary Mexican ideologies: machismo (discussed earlier) and indigenismo.

Indigenismo was a network of intellectual, cultural, and political discourses that argued that the roots of modern Mexican identity lay in the pre-Columbian Indian cultures that had been destroyed as a result

Figure 3.1. María Félix, as Rosaura the schoolteacher in *Río Escondido*, marches through the National Palace to her meeting with President Alemán. She represents the new Mexican woman who sacrifices her personal happiness for the nation. *Río Escondido*, production still.

of the Spanish conquest. However, the historian Alan Knight suggests that these postrevolutionary discourses about Indians "involved the imposition of ideas, categories, and policies from outside." According to Knight, the call for a unified national identity under the banner of a common Indian heritage was mobilized because those in power firmly believed that Indians could benefit from Mexico's growth only if they became fully integrated into the society from which they had previously been excluded. Indians thus became the "object" of indigenismo rather than its producer (Knight, 1990, 77).

Although the ideology of indigenismo purported to recognize the fundamental contribution of Indians to Mexican culture, its champions often failed to acknowledge linguistic, historical, and cultural differences, and even variations in racial stock among the diverse groups that made up Mexico's indigenous populations. This call for unity under the banner of a common Indian heritage was no more than a false ideology of an imagined alliance among ethnic, religious, and regional groups. This ambiguous context in which postrevolutionary Mexican nationalism was forged perhaps explains Mexico's continued search for an "authentic" national identity in political discourse and, subsequently, in Mexican cinema.

This search began in Mexico's nineteenth-century struggle for independence from Spain and France. Mexican intellectuals, while expounding an alternative to the culture of colonialism, asserted that "a common culture exists; diversity is merely superficial or epiphenomenal" (Schlesinger, 1987, 221). Their motive was to forge an identity that would either incorporate or erase diversity and at the same time to construct an "authentic" Mexican culture in opposition to European influences. However, in doing so, these political intellectuals ignored substantive historical differences based on gender, ethnicity, and culture.

In 1876, when General Porfirio Díaz came to power, the reigning social ideology was positivism, a philosophy of rational thought championed by writers and philosophers who referred to themselves as *los científicos*. These rationalists supported the Darwinian model of the survival of the fittest, promoted European culture while refusing Mexico's own indigenous influences, and advocated a "scientifically proven" masculine sovereignty. According to one prominent writer, Ignacio Gamboa, "men were morally and biologically superior to women" (quoted in Soto, 1990, 13).

While Díaz's administration established obligatory primary education for all male and female children, and higher schooling and vocational training for women became not only acceptable but also popular, at the same time divorce was outlawed, husbands retained all legal rights over property and children, and unmarried women under thirty could not leave their parental home without permission (Soto, 1990, 10).

The philosophical foundations of the Revolution of 1910 to 1920 were grounded in part in a rejection of both Díaz and positivism. Postrevolutionary Mexican intellectuals José Vasconcelos, Samuel Ramos, and Leopoldo Zea subsequently strove to rearticulate the historical, intellectual, cultural, and psychological roots of *mexicanidad* ("authentic" Mexicanness). The notion of a profoundly Mexican national identity emerged out of this concerted effort to discard the effects of European culture and to cast off the "mental chains of colonialism" (O'Malley, 1986, 110). However, this revised representation of the quintessential Mexican still described Mexican national identity as male and as non-Indian, effectively excluding a large segment of the Mexican population. Franco sums up the limits of mexicanidad by describing it as an "imagined nation."[4] Where, Franco asks, was woman in this new narrative (1992, 178)?

Scholars of Mexican history and culture, such as Eric R. Wolf, have argued that this revolutionary Mexican nationalism fed the same need as machismo in that it granted men the ability to "transcend the limits of the separate self," a self that was still exploited socially and economically, and "merge that self with a social body," the Mexican nation, separate from women (Wolf, 1959, 244).

Even before Octavio Paz affirmed Mexican identity to be male, Samuel Ramos came to similar conclusions in his long essay *Profile of Man and Culture*. In his analysis of the *pelado*, a derogatory term for a particularly unsavory male character of the lower classes, Ramos found "the most elemental and clearly defined expression of national character" whose "sexual organ becomes symbolic of masculine force" (1962, 58–60). While Ramos did not suggest that all Mexican men were pelados, his theorization of an "essential Mexican national identity" seemed determined to exclude a female identity.

Mexican Cinema and the Myth of Mexican Identity

Fernández maintained that his purpose as a filmmaker was to glorify Mexico, to counteract the thrust of Hollywood's influence on Mexican films, and to articulate and make sense of the past in order to reconstitute what he saw as an authentic Mexican national identity.[5] The Mexican feminist historian Julia Tuñón, however, argues that Fernández's "idea of Mexico was modified to fit his personal situation." She writes that "El Indio's" films "exalt" nationalism through their portrayal of a Mexico that "has nothing to do with a social construction or process . . . [but] is a sacred world, the terrain of beliefs and rituals" (1988, 164–165). Fernández's "sacred" Mexico was grounded in the complementary patriarchal discourses of indigenismo and machismo. Furthermore, as Tuñón puts it, Fernández's Mexico is a mythical essence that is fundamentally unalterable.

The narratives of both *María Candelaria* and *Río Escondido* confirm the existence of a rural Mexico that the historian Howard F. Cline situates at the "edge of the national economy and its political and social life" (1963, 111–112). According to Cline, while the marginal, mostly indigenous groups that populated these regions made up about 30 percent of Mexico's total population by 1950, they were so peripheral to the operations of the state that they "figure[d] at best as minor symbols in the political equations" (1963, 112). While most of Fernández's films focus on the "rural drama" and, according to Tuñón, appear to speak out "about the nation's hunger, about its ignorance, about the cacique's [a political boss] abuse of power . . . there appears the unconquerable force and inertia of an essential nature" (1988, 165).

While Fernández pictured himself as the cinematic savior of Mexico's downtrodden Indians (he was of Indian ancestry), his representations of these people, especially Indian women, were highly ambiguous. Women in these isolated rural communities were doubly oppressed, not only on the basis of class and ethnicity, but also because of their gender.[6] Although supposedly trying to find a place for Mexican woman in the discourse of national identity, Fernández's films instead reinforced women's confined position within the limits of Mexican patriarchy without revealing the social constraints that circumscribed these limits.

Figure 3.2. Fernández's Mexico was first and foremost Indian and rural. In collaboration with cinematographer Gabriel Figueroa, Fernández created a mythical Mexico of barren landscapes and endless, cloud-filled skies. *Río Escondido*, production still.

Two of the Mexican stars Fernández most often featured in his films to portray the essence of the Indian woman, María Félix and Dolores del Río, were light-skinned, European-looking women. And both functioned much like the female stars in the classical Hollywood cinema: clarifying cultural ideals of womanhood by redefining and reinforcing selective images of Mexican women and beauty, and thus of individual gendered identity.[7]

In 1942, Félix appeared in her first two films—*El peñón de las ánimas* (Miguel Zacarías), with Mexico's most popular male star, Jorge Negrete, and *María Eugenia* (Felipe Gregorio Castillo), under her maiden name, María de los Ángeles Félix. She became a top Mexican star the following year with her portrayal of the vengeful Doña Bárbara in the film of the same name. Félix's star status was affirmed in *Doña Bárbara*, and, as a result, she was afterward associated with this beautiful, but evil and aggressive, female character.[8]

Félix repeated her Doña Bárbara role of a powerful and wicked temptress, *la devoradora*, in a number of her subsequent films, such as *La mujer sin alma* (Fernando de Fuentes, 1943), *La devoradora* (Fuentes, 1946), and *La mujer de todos* (Bracho, 1946). Although Félix is most remembered for her roles as a femme fatale, she often played another kind of woman: for example, the rich but patriotic girl who marries the poor but brave revolutionary general in *Enamorada* (Fernández, 1946), the beautiful Indian girl in *Maclovia* (Fernández, 1948), and Rosaura, the self-sacrificing schoolteacher in *Río Escondido*.[9]

Del Río began her acting career in Hollywood, achieving star status in silent films such as Raoul Walsh's *What Price Glory* (1926). She eventually made over thirty films in Hollywood, including *The Girl of Rio* (1932), *Flying Down to Rio* (1933), and *The Fugitive* (1947). As Ana M. López has pointed out, del Río's otherness "did not have a specific national or ethnic provenance," and Hollywood was thus able to move her in and out of ethnic representations (1991b, 410). She played a Polynesian princess, a German spy, a Russian aristocrat, a French girl, a half-breed Indian, and a Brazilian dancer.

Del Río consistently refused requests to return to Mexico to star in Mexican films. However, in 1943, when her Hollywood career was declining and her lover, Orson Welles, had left her for Rita Hayworth, Fernández offered her the lead roles in *Flor silvestre* and *María Candelaria*. Del Río accepted his offer and returned to Mexico to play the role of a poor Indian girl who, for Fernández, symbolized Mexico.

María Candelaria

In *María Candelaria*,[10] del Río starred in the tragic story of a young Indian woman who is stoned to death by her own people. The plot of the film centers on María Candelaria, who lives outside the village of Xochimilco (City of the Floating Gardens) with her fiancé, Lorenzo

Rafael (Pedro Armendáriz), gathering and selling flowers to earn her livelihood. Because her mother was a prostitute, María is ostracized by the villagers and forced to live as an outcast.

María is constantly threatened by the mestizo Don Damian (Miguel Inclan) because she owes him money and because she refuses to be seduced by him. This narrative structuring device foregrounds relations of economic and social power that usually placed Indians at the mercy of mestizos and criollos. In the film, Don Damian, by virtue of his mixed blood, occupies a higher social position than the Indians. As the owner of the town's only general store, he controls their access to food, medicine, and other necessities. He also mediates their relations with the state. The government doctors deliver the antimalarial quinine to Don Damian to disperse to the Indians as he sees fit. "I make them take their medicine in front of me," he tells the doctors, "or they'd sell it or throw it away." Don Damian articulates the state's paternalistic attitude toward the Indians, who were generally considered to be like children, incapable of taking care of themselves.

After the opening credits, an intertitle, superimposed over the flowing water of Xochimilco, informs the audience that it is about to see "a romantic tragedy in a far-off indigenous corner of Mexico." The words "far-off" signal both a spatial and a temporal distance (the story takes place in a location and time far from the cinema theaters of the cities, from the social and economic problems of the 1940s, and from the everyday experiences of the audiences). A montage of pre-Columbian images illustrating this indigenous past ends with a shot of a young Indian woman standing next to the stone figure of an Aztec woman that has the same high cheekbones and proud facial expression as the live woman. While this shot is almost identical to one composed by Eisenstein for the prologue to his unfinished *Que viva México!*, it is not merely an isolated homage to the Soviet director. Tuñón has noted that when Fernández "imposes the monuments of Mexico's past upon the screen . . . he establishes them as living remains, a sign containing an eternal essence that goes beyond history" (1993, 167). Fernández's shot specifically links the past to the present through his representation of Mexico's "eternal" Indianness.

From this mythical past, the film dissolves to the present. In his studio, a famous Mexican painter (we never learn his name) is sur-

Figure 3.3. María Candelaria (Dolores del Río) with her fiancé, Lorenzo Rafael (Pedro Armendáriz). For the director, Fernández, who was of Indian ancestry, the roots of *lo mexicano*, the essential "Mexicanness," lay in Mexico's pre-Columbian past. *María Candelaria*, production still.

rounded by a group of students and journalists. When questioned about the themes of his work, he responds that he does not paint "themes," he paints his life, what he sees, and Mexico.

One of his visitors wants to view a portrait that has never been publicly exhibited. Reluctantly, the painter leads her up to his attic and uncovers the painting of an Indian woman. He describes her as "an

Indian of the pure Mexican race. . . . It was as if an old princess had come to judge the conquistadors." In opposition to Samuel Ramos and José Vasconcelos' theorization of the Mexican as a male mestizo, this film at first appears to locate national identity as Indian and as female, an attempt that will ultimately prove unsuccessful, however, due to the ideological limits of patriarchy, indigenismo, and Fernández's cinematic vision.

Set in 1909, one year before the outbreak of the Mexican Revolution, the film ignores the political and social pressures leading up to the protracted national conflict that profoundly reshaped Mexico and Mexico's idea of lo mexicano. Fernández instead characterized national identity as being rooted in Mexico's pre-Columbian heritage.

In María Candelaria, the themes of history, nation, and woman are tied together by Fernández's lyrical style and the film's mythical references to pre-Columbian Mexico. As discussed above, this theme of the Indian as the link between past and present was central to Mexican historical discourse and Mexican cinema. In the 1930s, films such as Janitzio (Carlos Navarro, 1934) and Redes (Agustín Velazques, Paul Strand, and Fred Zinneman, 1934) initiated the "Indianist" genre. While glorifying both an Indian past and the Indian people, these films did not concern themselves with the fact that these people were Mexico's most exploited group, persecuted on the basis of race as well as class.

After the opening scene described above, the painter begins to narrate the film's plot. Sarah Kozloff describes this kind of narrator as "embedded," in that the narrating character's role in a film is specifically connected to the narrative project (1989, 50). The film in fact starts to unfold as a retelling of the painter's encounter with María. He places the story in a specific geographic and temporal frame, grounds it in historical reality, and makes it seem true by his act of remembering.

However, the flashback structure only pretends to allow the film to be a narrated fable about a young Indian woman who is misunderstood by her people. The authority of the painter's voice in María Candelaria configures another story: that of a man's attempt to absolve himself for his failure to prevent a woman's death.

Maureen Turim has demonstrated that film flashbacks often serve as a cinematic link between the present and the past, working to reveal how individuals select, order, and make sense of memories (1989, 2). In this sense, the telling of *María Candelaria* may be seen as a strategy for reshaping history from the point of view of individual, selective memory, which in this film belongs to a man.

However, *María Candelaria* does not follow the usual pattern of the narrated film: the painter is physically absent for most of the narrative and, moreover, after the opening scene, his narrative voice does not reemerge until the last scene of the film. If he did not figure as a central character in the film, his absence would be understandable. But, according to "his" plot, his presence is central to development of the narrative.

According to Shlomith Rimmon-Kenan, while a narrator who does not participate in the story is accorded the power of omniscience, or narrational authority, narrators who occupy a central or peripheral role in the narrative may be characterized by a certain degree of "unreliability" (1983, 94–103). Rimmon-Kenan writes that "the main sources of unreliability are the narrator's limited knowledge, his personal involvement, and his problematic value-scheme" (1983, 100). The painter in *María Candelaria* fulfills this definition of an "unreliable" narrator, thus forcing us to question his version of history.

He is absent for most of the film and therefore would seem to have limited access to the plot's unfolding. David Bordwell argues that the use of individual memory in this kind of situation works to motivate a "shift in chronology," but in the case of *María Candelaria*, the painter's uninformed memory also functions as an attempt by a man to appropriate a woman's story. However, despite the authority of the painter's voice and his role in bringing about María's death, it is the woman's story that the narrative traces, and it is woman who emerges as the central figure in this narrative about national identity.

The painter first sees María at the local market. Exclaiming to himself and to the spectator, "That is the woman I have been searching for," he asks her to pose for him. He wants to possess her, he implies, so that he may represent her as "the essence of [Mexican] beauty." This "innocent" expression of male desire is an example of the enigmatic nature of patriarchy, which seeks complete psychic and material possession of woman. However, as will be seen, this "possession" is a complex process that is not wholly successful in *María Candelaria*.

While the explicit function of the painting in the first scene of *María*

Candelaria is to further the narrative (the painting initiates the telling of the film's story), it also is a sign of the constructed nature of desire and of representation. Although the painting itself is never seen, its centrality to the painter's desire, and thus to the development of the narrative, emphasizes the split between reality and the portrayal of reality in painting and in film.

The painting is not a "realistic" representation of María or of any particular woman. According to the film, it is actually a painting of one woman's face and another woman's body. After drawing María's face, the painter is forced to recruit another model when María runs off, refusing to pose naked. However, this is not a major problem for the painter. His intention, after all, is merely to paint the "essence" of the beauty of the Mexican Indian woman.

The painting of the naked woman is eventually discovered, and an angry mob of her own people chase María through the streets of the town, eventually stoning her to death. According to the film, María is killed for two reasons: First, she violated moral customs. By posing for the painter, the Indians believed María exposed her body to a man who was not her husband. Second, they believed that María did this willingly and for personal and selfish reasons: to collect enough money so that she and Lorenzo Rafael could be married.

On the one hand, María Candelaria may be read as a story of a man's attempt to situate himself in both a personal and a national history. As an intellectual, the painter positions himself as an observer and privileged interpreter of the lives of the masses. As he begins his narrative, he expresses his horror and pain at the process of retelling the story. What remains unclear, however, is whether this reflection emerges in response to María's fate or to his own repressed guilt.

The apparent purpose of the painter's narrative may thus be seen as an attempt to find personal meaning in the complex workings of history. As Paz puts it, "the grandeur of man [sic] consists in his making beautiful and lasting works out of the real substance of that nightmare [history] . . . transforming the nightmare into vision," in order to free oneself from the "shapeless horror of reality" (1985, 104).

However, besides the level of the individual unconscious, there is another level on which this narrative works, through what Fredric Jameson defines as the "political unconscious." If we consider this level, we find a number of conflicted historical themes that extend beyond the personal to involve the Spanish conquest, the Mexican Revolution, and the historical quest for an essential Mexican national identity.

If woman is defined foremost by her body, then any attempt by patriarchy to control that definition, through discourse or through painterly or cinematic representation, implies an attempt to control and possess that body. According to psychoanalytic theory, the desire to possess something is prompted by a feeling of "lack" on the part of the one who desires. If we examine the painter's desire to paint or to represent María, we must ask, What is the missing object that induced this expression? I will suggest that in the context of the "political unconscious" of Mexico in the 1940s, as expressed in this film, the object is national identity, specifically, a place for woman in the expression of this identity.

As suggested above, through the representation of the oppressive relations between the mestizos and the Indians, the film may first of all be seen as another in a long line of narratives about the complex processes that destroyed Mexico's indigenous cultures. Second, María's murder dramatizes a cinematic attempt at narratively reconstructing the La Malinche paradigm and the story of La Malinche's relation to Mexican history. In this version, the María/La Malinche figure can be seen as a martyr to Mexico's death (the Spanish conquest) and rebirth (the Mexican Revolution).

If, as Ramirez Berg suggests, Indians are "Mexican cinema's structured absence" as well as its "inescapable other," then María, as an Indian woman, is doubly oppressed on the basis of ethnicity as well as gender (1992a, 130). Like La Malinche, she functions in this film as an intermediary between the Indians and their oppressors. And, like La Malinche, María is forced to betray her people in order to save them: she must model for the painter in order to get enough money to free Lorenzo Rafael from prison.

At the conclusion of the story, the painter offers neither a moral, a summary, nor a personal reflection. Instead, his final voice-over affirms merely that "this was the story of María Candelaria," thereby establishing the fable as truth and stopping further investigation of his relation to the murder, on one level, and his connection, as a criollo, to historical genocide, on another. By trying to capture a personal event as emblematic of a mythical history, the narrative has avoided the larger consideration of the ideological and physical oppression of both Indians and women.

The film does not evaluate the painter's position vis-à-vis historical relations of gender, class, and race. By intervening in María's life (through his representation of her), the painter ultimately contributes to her tragic death. On an allegorical level, *María Candelaria* may thus be read as a narrative attempt to absolve the criollo's guilt for his part in the destruction of Mexico's indigenous cultures by reminding Mexico that it was an Indian woman, La Malinche, who betrayed the Mexicans.[11] However, it is almost as if the painter's role in this narrative does not matter anymore. Through her tragic death, the story has become María's. The man's interpretive process is interrupted and his personal memory is repressed. Although the film is narrated by a man, national identity is ultimately configured through identification with an Indian woman who tried to save her people, thus reconstructing, if only momentarily, the La Malinche paradigm.

Río Escondido

Fernández's later film, *Río Escondido*, which won the Academia Mexicana de Ciencias y Artes Cinematográficas awards for best picture, best director, best cinematography, and best actress in 1947 (García Riera, 1969, V, 176), explores the same themes of national identity and gender as *María Candelaria* but does so within the context of the 1940s. It is the story of an idealistic young teacher named Rosaura (María Félix), who had wanted to be a doctor until a bad heart forced her to abandon her studies and become a teacher.

Public education for all classes had been one of the principal goals of nationalism since the immediate postrevolutionary period. José Vasconcelos, minister of education in the 1920s, advocated a universal literacy program that involved hundreds of young women who, like Rosaura, were sent into the countryside to teach. This practice continued into the 1940s.

At the beginning of the film, Rosaura is personally assigned by President Miguel Alemán to a remote area in northern Mexico, with instructions to bring education and civilization to an illiterate Indian

Figure 3.4. Rosaura stands in for the Virgin of Guadalupe, Mexico's indigenous Virgin Mary. Her role is to provide spiritual relief to the economically poor and politically exploited residents of Río Escondido. *Río Escondido,* production still.

population. Her secondary duty is to mediate and promote the political project of the nation. The Indians that Rosaura must raise out of ignorance into modernity still live within the prerevolutionary social structure of the *caciquismo*.[12] Appointed *caciques* (bosses) functioned in rural agricultural cooperatives as representatives of the state's authority, much like the traditional don of the hacienda in the eighteenth and nineteenth centuries. Although ostensibly the role of these bosses was to promote "popular participation in national politics" at the rural level, James Cockcroft argues that caciquismo was the "basic cause" of the state's failure to incorporate the lower-class rural masses into effective political participation. Cockcroft writes that "*caciquismo* and its system of bribes, payoffs, and control has thus served to disguise or divert the heightened stratification and conflict within the rural population it buttresses" (1983, 203–204).

Rosaura arrives in the village of Río Escondido to find Don Regino, the cruel cacique, attempting to break a horse. When the horse throws him, he beats the animal savagely. Rosaura tries to stop him, but he throws her violently to the ground. As the cacique raises his whip to beat her, he is challenged by an elderly Indian man. Don Regino responds by whipping the man instead. This is Rosaura's introduction to rural Mexico, where, twenty years after the end of the Revolution, machismo is still in power and relations between men are still predicated on class and race.

Not all of the caciques were corrupt, but many of them, like the powerful and cruel boss of Río Escondido, appropriated more than their share of political, economic, and social power within their small empires. Though the film takes place in 1947, time seems to have stopped in this isolated region of northern Mexico. The Indians of the poor, rural village of Río Escondido exist outside of history. In this film, the Mexican Revolution has never touched the lives of Mexico's Indians, except to substitute one oppressor for another.

With the help of a young doctor she meets at the Presidential Palace, Rosaura manages to destroy Don Regino and to bring modernity—in the form of medicine, clean water, and an end to caciquismo —to the Indians. However, like María Candelaria, Rosaura must sacrifice her life to pay for what she has done.

On a narrative level, Rosaura's journey to the Río Escondido area signifies the state's attempt to incorporate the uneducated, poverty-stricken rural masses into modern Mexico. According to Susan De-ver, this area of "primitive" Mexico was thematized in Mexican cinema as an "impediment" to nation-building (1992, 57). Using teachers like Rosaura, the government offers to pull these forgotten people up through secular and political education. Substituting the rhetoric of indigenismo for economic and social reform, however, does not offer the indigenous people material sustenance or apologies for four hundred years of subjugation. Though the film suggests that Indians may be guided toward political consciousness by the sacrifice of a single courageous woman, by the end of the film little in the way of material comfort has been delivered to the people of Río Escondido.

In contrast to the general trajectory of development in most Western countries, growth and modernization in Latin American countries were marked by uneven development. Modernization occurred at different rates and in different periods in various geographic regions and among distinct populations in countries such as Mexico, Brazil, and Peru.[13] *Río Escondido* dramatized this opposition between modernity and underdevelopment through its representation of the hurried pace of politicians, doctors, and businessmen in the city and the slow, measured, and repetitive motions of subsistence living and ritual practices in the isolated Mexican feudal communities in the late 1940s.

While Bartra argues that what he calls "the re-creation of agrarian history" is the "keystone" in the myth of the Mexican nation, places like Río Escondido did exist, isolated not only by their physical remoteness from the cities, but also through their social and cultural distance from the industrial, agricultural, and discursive centers of the nation in the 1940s.

Describing certain Hollywood films from the 1940s that portrayed comparable traditional and rural spaces, Dana Polan suggests that such "pastoral" locations "represent the unproductive places left behind in modernity's expansion" (1986, 267). For Polan, the significance of acknowledging these kinds of spatial and social separations in film narratives lies in the recognition that at any specific historical moment, there exist a "variety of narrational options" that must be considered (1986, 33): "In writing history, we don't write so much *the* meaning of the period as a history of some *possible* meanings," which are based on a reading of the relation among historically specific social grids (Polan, 1986, 10).

In Mexico, as noted above, the "story" of the nation was not a single narrative of economic development but a montage of narratives, each differing in structure and content but connected through what Polan defines as a "gridding" of social discourse or what Bartra calls "mythical networks of political power." The official narrative of the Revolution described how social and economic benefits were provided for Mexico's diverse population. However, by 1947, the social changes the Revolution had promised to deliver to all Mexicans were nearly forgotten in the rush toward economic development. There arose other, conflicting narratives that recounted the relation of disenfranchised groups—women and Indians—to this new national configuration. Rosaura's role in *Río Escondido* is to reassure Mexico's marginalized groups that the Revolution is still responding to the needs of the poor, the downtrodden, the illiterate, and women.

Rosaura's weak heart, which prevented her from becoming a doctor, also functions to reinforce the idea of the inherent weakness of woman. Because of this weakness, Rosaura cannot ultimately succeed in her mission without help from the male doctor, Felipe. It is Felipe who cures Don Regino when he becomes sick and, in exchange, receives permission to inoculate the Indians. And it is Felipe who gives Rosaura the gun that temporarily saves her life and her virginity. When Don Regino attempts to rape Rosaura for refusing to become his mistress, she kills him with this gun as his men and the Indians stand outside the house, listening to her screams. Though maintaining her virginity, Rosaura succumbs to her weak heart as a result of Don Regino's assault. As she lies dying, Felipe rushes in with a personal letter of thanks from President Alemán for her unselfish work in the name of *la patria*.

Dever argues that "Fernández's choice of Félix—so long identified as a 'savage man hater' . . . underscores the transformation of the independent woman to dutiful charge of the state" (1992, 59). However, although Rosaura eventually dies in the line of duty, she does emerge in this film, despite the will of the state, as *the* primary destroyer of oppression and machismo. When Don Regino stumbles out the door and falls to the ground, the Indians, mobilized by Rosaura's courageous moral example, descend upon his army with sticks and flaming torches. Perhaps Fernández's choice of the "savage man hater" was not as ambiguous as Dever suggests.

Montage, Ideology, and Representation

One of the major cinematic influences on Fernández's style was the work of Eisenstein. This influence is most evident in Fernández's use of montage as a narrative and representational strategy and through his incorporation of contradictory compositional elements within the frame.

Fernández used these Eisensteinian strategies to articulate various relations between Mexican identity, Mexican history, and Mexico as a physical and geographic space. In addition, Ramirez Berg argues that Fernández's montages are similar to those of Eisenstein in that they "are often graphic representations of . . . divisive social and ideological practices that Fernández-Figueroa protagonists seek to defeat" (1992b, 35).

The opening title montage of *Río Escondido* offers an example of Fernández's ideological use of montage. The sequence contextualizes the film's story of the heroic struggle of a self-sacrificing young teacher who renounces her own life to bring hope to a handful of Indians living, almost forgotten, in northern Mexico. The titles, superimposed over a series of commissioned engravings by the Mexican artist Leopoldo Méndez, preview the film's plot while attempting to narrate the whole of Mexican history and foretell the country's future (Dever, 1992, 58).

The engravings, which at first glance seem to trace Mexico's emergence from oppression to freedom, also evidence an attempt to reincorporate women and Indians into the discourse of national identity. For example, the first engraving, an image of the lighted torch of "knowledge and freedom," is followed by a shot of a woman's figure silhouetted against a Mexican landscape, a juxtaposition that firmly ties woman to the nation.

Conversely, men are represented in this montage as the perpetrators of oppression. An image of a man's booted feet resting on the top of a table covered with liquor bottles and glasses, followed by the engraving of a child sitting by the figure of his sick mother, suggests that the brutal heel of patriarchal oppression has resulted in the suffering of women and children. A subsequent representation of armed men standing around the figure of a dead Indian, followed by the image of a naked Indian on his knees, entreating his gods to save him, portrays the brutal destruction of Mexico's indigenous peoples by lawless and godless men. And, finally, the engraving of an old, gnarled tree suggests that through all this history, Mexico survives—and so will the "good Mexicans," who are presented as women and Indians.

After this introduction, the film dissolves to shots of Mexico City that emphasize its modernity and its distance from the country's isolated rural communities. We first see Rosaura hurrying up the steps of the Presidential Palace, where she receives her orders directly from President Alemán. With her personal mandate in hand, she boards the train to Ciudad Juárez. The following sequence is one of most famous in Mexican cinematic history and offers a synthesis of Fernández and Figueroa's cinematic style. The scene, composed of five shots of the isolated and inhospitable deserts of northern Mexico, highlights the differences between Mexico's urban and rural landscapes and suggests that life in this remote area is quite unlike life in the cities. The sequence lasts for five minutes; no dialogue interrupts the visual message, and Rosaura remains the only human figure in a barren landscape.

Although dialectical divisions are visually represented as light versus dark and foreground versus background, montage in Fernández's films also takes on the form of binary opposition based on sexual difference. Judith Mayne has noted a similar effect in many early Soviet films. She argues that this opposition is not necessarily grounded in a portrayal of male and female, but in qualities she defines as abstract and concrete, or passive versus active, qualities that align themselves discursively as female versus male. While most histories of Soviet cinema suggest that filmmakers and critics like Kuleshov, Eisenstein, and Vertov developed cinematic montage as a specifically political aesthetic, Mayne argues that dialectic montage also presents a formal situation in which "the drama of opposition between the poles of activity and passivity is reenacted." Moreover, she finds that in many of the Soviet films of the 1920s, these oppositions take the form of sexual difference that are repeatedly portrayed as "natural" (1989, 31–34).[14]

A similar strategy may be observed in Fernández's films. Ramirez

Berg has remarked at length on Fernández's use of diagonal lines in his cinematic compositions and compares this approach to Eisenstein's utilization of diagonals to signify social imbalance. For example, Ramirez Berg suggests that the repeated use of the diagonal in the montage that depicts Rosaura's journey to Río Escondido "foreshadows the unbalanced social order she [Rosaura] is entering" (1992b, 36).

The first shot of this sequence features a low-angle close-up of Rosaura framed against the cloud-filled sky. She turns and walks toward the horizon, away from the stationary camera. A mountain range is faintly visible in the distance, but other than Rosaura's figure, the only element in the frame is a solitary cactus. The use of a long lens flattens distance, but at the same time makes Rosaura's retreating figure seem to grow smaller quickly. She is enveloped by the harsh Mexican landscape that seems to offer little sustenance to any living creature.

This shot dissolves to another very similar shot of Rosaura in the distance, still walking slowly toward the mountains. However, in this shot the trajectory of her path bisects the frame at a diagonal. In both shots, the horizon splits the frame across the lower third of the screen. The film then cuts to an empty landscape. After a beat, Rosaura enters from screen right and walks at a slight diagonal toward the camera. The camera pans with her to keep her on the right edge of the composition, and her figure enlarges quickly as she approaches the frontal plane of the frame. She stops for a moment, looks offscreen, then exits screen left.

Next, in another very low-angle shot, Rosaura again enters from screen right. There is no visible horizon in this framing, and she walks away from the camera on a diagonal, toward the top left corner of the frame. In the following shot, she walks toward the camera. This time, the horizon bisects the frame at an extreme diagonal. Rosaura walks very slowly toward a cactus in the lower right corner of the frame and finally collapses next to it.

While I find Ramirez Berg's analysis perceptive, it is incomplete in that it does not consider the way in which gender is represented by the diagonal motif. In her analysis of Eisenstein's film *October*, Mayne argues that in addition to considering the ideological function of montage and compositional motifs within specific shots and within the structure of the entire film, it is also necessary to look at how these "visual structures . . . represent women" (1989, 4). In the case of *Río Escondido*, and in the above montage in particular, it is a woman who causes a disruption in the visual composition of the frame, in the logical composition of the narrative, and, ultimately, in the social ideology of nationalism.

The dialectic of male/female is also structured into the thematics of both *Río Escondido* and *María Candelaria*, where, for example, women are metaphorically aligned with nature and men with society—and, moreover, this alignment is presented as natural.[15] María is continually compared with water, animals, and plant life: she sells flowers for a living; a pig and its piglets bring her the resources for her marriage; and the rivers of Xochimilco carry her through life and toward the afterlife. As an element of nature, María is placed in opposition to male civilization, represented on the one hand by the mestizo Don Damian, who destroys nature, and on the other hand by the painter, who, as an artist, produces and preserves it. This tactic further legitimizes the supposedly natural roots of both Indian and woman.

Rosaura is similarly represented. The montage analyzed above situates her as part of Mexico's indigenous landscape and suggests that woman shares certain qualities of nativity, remoteness, and permanence with this landscape. In a number of shots in *Río Escondido*, Rosaura is silhouetted against a tree or a cactus. These two figures, framed against Figueroa's mythical Mexican sky, are the only objects in the shot.

Reimagining the Virgin

María and Rosaura are aligned both visually and symbolically with the Virgin Mary. María represents the Virgin's holiness and virginal status. After Lorenzo is dragged away by Don Damian's henchmen, María cries at the foot of the Virgin's statue inside the church. As she looks lovingly up at this icon of perfect femininity, the camera frames them in a single shot, their heads covered with dark rebozos, their hands placed together in an attitude of prayer, and their eyes filled with tears.

Rosaura represents the motherly and virginal aspects of the Virgin Mary. First, she assumes a motherly role toward the Indians, who are portrayed as naive children. Soon after her arrival, Rosaura adopts three children whose mother was one of the first to die in a smallpox

Figure 3.5. In both *Río Escondido* and *María Candelaria*, women embody spiritual power. In a number of shots and in the narratives of these two films, Rosaura and María are aligned with the Virgin Mary, with the Christ figure, or with the Church. *Río Escondido*, production still.

epidemic. Although a potential romantic relationship between Rosaura and Felipe is hinted at, it never develops. Rosaura must sacrifice all personal attachments and remain a virgin for the benefit of the nation. And, finally, the schoolroom in *Río Escondido*, presented as the space of Mexico's future, is displayed as a space controlled by woman. One of the few paths to national identity open to a woman, besides motherhood, apparently was teaching.

María and Rosaura are also compared to the Virgin Mary in terms of goodness, purity, and sacrifice, and it is their spiritual power (rather than their social power) that ultimately defines their identity as Mexican. It is within this space of moral sacrifice that they may contribute to Mexico's future. Just as the Indian Virgin of Guadalupe functioned as a moral figure, so, too, these films portray woman as Mexico's moral conscience by restoring the meaning and power of Catholicism, which, according to Fernández's representations, had been devitalized by the institution of the Church.

Although the Revolution was ideologically anticlerical, Indians and other lower-class Mexicans retained a strong connection to Catholicism. At the same time, while decrying the power of the Church, the Revolution's leaders often used it and its priests as intermediaries in the transition from one paternal system to what would eventually become another paternal relation between the rulers and their subjects.[16]

The Church figures prominently in *María Candelaria* and *Río Escondido*, as it does in many of Fernández's films. Jean Franco finds that in Fernández's film *Enamorada* (released just prior to *Río Escondido* in 1947), the Church serves both a political and an ideological role, functioning as a "mediator between the old landowning class and the new revolutionary leadership, and between the sexes" (1989, 149). However, in *María Candelaria* and *Río Escondido*, it is woman who mediates the various ideological shifts in relations of class, gender, and race. While the Church, and its representative the priest, may mediate between the individual and God, they are both ultimately ineffective in arbitrating between humans.[17] According to the narrative of *Río Escondido*, Rosaura's short stay in Río Escondido destroys the oppressive, feudal Mexican hacienda system and restores the "natural" balance between the Indians, the nation, and the Church.

The alignment of woman, nature, and spirituality with the past in *Río Escondido* and *María Candelaria* works to position women as initiators of moral reformation rather than social and economic change. These film melodramas of the 1940s projected a certain conception of the "moral universe" that women were required both to clarify and to uphold in support of national reformation.

Machismo and the Nation in *María Candelaria* and *Río Escondido*

Feminists have suggested that male characters often function in film as representatives of the dominant classes. However, a number of different forms of masculinity are portrayed in *María Candelaria* and *Río Escondido*. María and Rosaura are each pitted against a male mestizo character who represents the worst of Mexican machismo. The violent treatment of women and Indians by these *malos mexicanos* is emphasized in these films because the men's actions are supposedly contrary to the nationalist ideology of a peaceful assimilation of all peoples into a new definition of the nation.

In *Río Escondido* this negative side of machismo is personified by Don Regino, a cruel and despotic drunkard who beats horses, women, and old men for no apparent reason. His worst crime, however, is that he has abandoned the Revolution for personal power separate from the aims of the national government. Because Río Escondido is so far from Mexico City, it exists as if it were its own feudal state, ruled by the immediate power figure of Don Regino. Through his violent and dictatorial reinforcement of paternalism, Don Regino represents all that is wrong with traditional machismo.

His personal "army" is made up of mestizos who are pitted against the Indians, and Don Regino runs Río Escondido as a mini-state. Thus, when Rosaura points out that she has been sent by the president of Mexico, the cacique proudly asserts, "Here, there is no other president than me." Don Regino has no use for modernity's revision of women's social role. He had forced the previous schoolteacher, an Indian woman, to be his mistress, and he expects this of Rosaura as well. He will rebuild her school and provide water for the Indians on the condition that she move into his house. When she resists, he revokes any public commitments he made to the villagers and blames Rosaura for his action.

Dr. Felipe, called to Río Escondido by Rosaura to combat a smallpox epidemic, represents another, more benevolent side of paternalism and machismo. His role is to prove to the Indians that they need the protection of the government against the malos mexicanos as well as such misfortunes as disease, poverty, and illiteracy. While the doctor personifies a positive aspect of patriarchy, his social position is still above that of Rosaura and the Indians.

The absent figure of the Indian hero Benito Juárez is offered as yet another symbol of Mexican paternalism. Juárez, a leader of Mexico's Liberal Reform movement (1855–1867), is employed by Fernández (himself of Indian ancestry) as a model for what Indians *could be* for Mexico. This incorporation of Juárez represents part of a continuing nationalist project to remind the Indians of their connection to the ongoing ideological project of the nation's Revolution. However, what is left out of this rhetoric is that the Juarista administration was funda-

Figure 3.6. Fernández's films presented various figures of machismo. Dr. Felipe (Fernando Fernández) in *Río Escondido* represents the benevolent Mexican man who takes care of his social inferiors, women, and Indians. *Río Escondido*, production still.

mentally antiunion. As Cockcroft puts it, Juárez turned peasants into free wage labor by "dispossessing them of their lands," thus laying "the foundations in both urban and rural areas for a speedier development of capitalist forms of production" and ensuring an abundant and cheap labor pool (1983, 80). *Río Escondido* leaves most of these troubling aspects of Juárez's politics out of its history lesson. Rosaura describes Juárez to the Indian schoolchildren as "a defender of the poor against the bad Mexicans," thus separating off a certain portion of Mexicans who alone were supposedly responsible for Mexico's history of Indian oppression.

These various constructions of masculinity in both *María Cande-*

Figure 3.7. Lorenzo Rafael symbolizes another kind of macho. Denied the political and economic privileges of the upper class, he is nevertheless granted the man's privilege over women. *María Candelaria*, production still.

laria and *Río Escondido* confirm the unequal relations between men and women in Mexican ideology and practice in the 1940s. While clarifying local feelings on morality, the struggle between the painter and Lorenzo in *María Candelaria* over the right to desire and possess María also illustrates that machismo easily crosses boundaries of class and race. María is not given the chance to respond to the painter's request before Lorenzo, offended by the painter's appeal, drags her away from the market. For Fernández's men, whether a white member of the upper-class intelligentsia or a poor Indian, women are objects to be owned, struggled over, and traded, as La Malinche was.

Fernández claimed that he looked to narrative and aesthetic traditions in Mexican art in order to develop what he hoped would become an authentic Mexican cinema.[18] His fundamental intention was not to create new kinds of cinematic strategies but to create a cinema that explored Mexican cultural, social, and historical issues. However, as discussed above, his films instead often repressed the analysis of the historical forces that shaped cultural and social differences.

Bartra suggests that writers and film directors like Fernández, who purported to be involved in the nationalist project, played a crucial educational role in legitimizing the existing system. While Fernández may have believed that his films were Mexican because they incorporated certain aspects of traditional culture, Bartra argues that such mediations "give rise to a paradox" in which both film directors and their audience accept and applaud the contradictions between "the reality they perceive and the films they produce" (1992, 171–172). Despite this contract between producers and consumers, these films could not successfully integrate new representations into narratives of change because they refused to deal with fundamental psychic and historical structures that sustained Mexican patriarchy.

María and Rosaura are ultimately sacrificed because of the (unconscious) inability of Mexican films to deal with a possible transformation of women's position in narrative structures, just as Mexican society was unable to integrate women into its shifting structures of nation and national identity. However, both characters function as central narrative agents who make a difference in the lives of the people around them, in the narratives of Mexican cinema, and in the narratives of social discourse about woman and national identity.

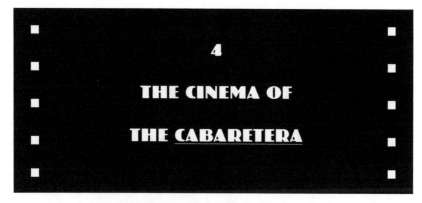

4

THE CINEMA OF

THE CABARETERA

Around us are bronze men in blue outfits . . .
cheap rings worn on labor-hardened fingers wink with false
brilliance at the equally cheap earrings in the ears of bronze girls.
Their power—and the lilac shade which it lends to bronze skin—
seems in the blue and red neon light like a sore on the cheeks. . . .
Drooping paper flowers, white teeth splitting dark faces
with a smile. A black eye. A naked shoulder—all black and blue.
A neck covered with bite marks. A blood-red bruise.

Sergei Eisenstein

The 1940s was the decade of the cabaretera (dance-hall) film in Mexican cinema. Though similar to Hollywood's "fallen women" film, the cabaretera was clearly a Mexican genre that incorporated aspects of the earlier "seduced and abandoned" Mexican melodramas, hard-edged elements of the *cine de arrabal* (Mexican cinema's urban melodrama), and popular music from the tropics: the Cuban *danzón*, the rumba, and the Brazilian samba.[1] Like the Hollywood genre, Mexico's fallen-women films emerged as a response to changes in social and economic roles for women and the resulting difficulty of incorporating these changes into patriarchal discourse about female sexuality.

The films of the cine de arrabal and the cabaretera were set in the poor urban barrios of Mexico City, which were expanding as a result of the migration of campesinos into the cities in search of work. While Mexico was experiencing an unprecedented economic expansion in certain sectors of society, most people still earned their meager

Figure 4.1. The cabaretera genre spoke to a rapidly expanding urban audience. These films portrayed the lives of the large underclass with a combination of gritty realism and Mexican cinematic melodrama. *Salón México*, advertising poster.

incomes from agricultural work. At the same time, a rapidly expanding class of workers, intellectuals, and small-business owners was struggling to make a living in overcrowded cities. Stories for these urban melodramas, often adapted from newspaper articles and popular fiction, focused on the lives of struggling workers and their families.

One of the central issues for Mexican society at this time was the increasing recognition of the failure of the Mexican Revolution to bring social and economic rewards to the lower classes, the indigenous populations, and women. The heroes of the cine de arrabal were men of these lower classes, who, according to the films, incorporated all the elements of the "authentic" Mexican. They were resourceful individuals who somehow managed to rise above the constraints of poverty—morally, if not economically.

While the principal characters of the cine de arrabal were male, the cabaretera films centered on a female character. As described above by Eisenstein, the Mexican cabareteras were spaces that foregrounded desire and sexuality; in fact, the cabaretera was one site in which female sexuality could be expressed in Mexican society. Typically, the protagonists of the 1940s cabareteras were women supporting their families in one of the few lucrative positions available to them. Called *las ficheras*, many of these women were in fact prostitutes. While a number of films about prostitutes had been produced in the 1930s, beginning with *Santa* in 1931, the cabaretera films of the Ávila Camacho and Alemán eras were more pessimistic and reflected a world consumed with the anxieties of social transformation. Carl J. Mora draws a link between this increased anxiety and the cabaretera, writing that "the unabashed greed given free rein by Alemán's ambitious developmentalist regime created severe societal stresses that found expression" in these films about prostitutes (1989, 87).

The cabaretera attempted to update the La Malinche paradigm of the "bad woman" in order to assimilate the Mexican working-class woman whose newfound social and economic power challenged the male's traditional position of superiority. This chapter will examine two cabaretera films of the 1940s—Julio Bracho's *Distinto amanecer* (*A New Morning*, 1943) and Emilio Fernández's *Salón México* (*The Mexican Ballroom*, 1947)—both of which focused on the conflicted position of woman in Mexico during the postrevolutionary drive for economic development on the national level and economic survival on the personal level.

Modernity, Ideology, and Desire

In 1905 there were 11,554 legally registered prostitutes in Mexico City, which had a total population of about 368,000 (Turner, 1968, 191). After

1910, the number of prostitutes increased dramatically due to the economic and social devastation caused by war and the migration of large numbers of unskilled rural peasants to the cities in search of work. The cinematic *época de las cabareteras* is thus a comment not only about prostitution but also on the effects of "urbanization and modernity" (Sánchez, 1989, 55).

The few fallen-woman films released in the 1930s were typically concerned with an innocent young girl like Santa, who is seduced, abandoned, and forced, out of shame and economic necessity, into a life of prostitution. In Arcady Boytler's tragic melodrama *La mujer del puerto* (*Woman of the Port*, 1933), based on a story by Guy de Maupassant, Rosario (Andrea Palma) becomes a prostitute after her father is killed by her unfaithful fiancé. While working at a brothel in the eastern port city of Veracruz, Rosario unknowingly sleeps with her long-lost brother (Domingo Soler). Upon learning what she has done, she throws herself into the ocean in remorse.

Although no longer the innocent girl of *Santa* or *La mujer del puerto*, the protagonist of the dance-hall films of the 1940s remains a sympathetic character, a good woman forced into a bad life by circumstances beyond her control. In Fernández's precursor to *Salón México*, *Las abandonadas* (*The Abandoned Women*, 1944), for example, Dolores del Río sacrifices her own happiness for the sake of her son. Similarly, Libertad Lamarque plays the title role in *Soledad* (Tito Davidson, 1948), the story of a servant (Lamarque) in love with the son of the wealthy family she works for. Forced into marriage, impregnated, and then abandoned, Lamarque's character sacrifices her own happiness for her daughter. These women emerge as self-sufficient characters who often manage to rise above their fate, if only momentarily.

As discussed earlier, the social and economic reorganization Mexico faced in the 1940s affected both class relations and relations between the sexes. On the one hand, Mexican women faced significant changes in all aspects of their lives, and on the other hand, nationalist discourses stressed the importance of preserving traditional values of motherhood, chastity, and obedience. These conflicting demands were difficult to negotiate for both men and women. Although the cabaretera films dramatized the tensions surrounding the roles assigned to Mexican women in the 1940s, and some even offered positive por-

Figure 4.2. The Mexican cabaretera genre dramatized the lives of women forced into prostitution through no fault of their own. However, these films failed to interrogate the social and economic circumstances that required good women to become bad. *Santa*, production still.

trayals of women, at the same time the films had a difficult time providing narrative resolutions for material conflicts.

Julio Bracho's *Distinto amanecer* dramatizes the effects of these conflicts within the context of emergent feminism and the disintegration of the Mexican family. The film traces the events during an unexpected reunion one night of three intellectuals who many years before, as students, had been politically active in the Revolution. The female protagonist, Julieta (Andrea Palma), works as a dance-hall hostess in order

Figure 4.3. This shot from *Distinto amanecer* illustrates the effects of unprecedented economic expansion in Mexico in the 1940s. In the new urban spaces, tradition mixes with modernity and the indigenous mixes with the foreign, offering Mexicans social choices they never had before. *Distinto amanecer,* production still.

to support her younger brother, Juanito, and her husband, Ignacio (Alberto Galán). When the intrusion of an old boyfriend, Octavio (Pedro Armendáriz), into their lives threatens the fragile stability of their family, Julieta is forced to confront the dilemma of whether to stay in a loveless marriage with her husband or run off with Octavio. Her struggle to come to a decision threatens the film's narrative coherence and calls into question the ideological positions of Mexican women in the 1940s.

While Ramirez Berg suggests that, in general, the Golden Age films created an "idealized, romanticized, and imaginary Mexico," this film, in contrast, offers a darker, bleaker picture of postrevolutionary Mexico (1992a, 15). Depicting urban society as a threatening and decaying world populated by beggars, prostitutes, and corrupt political functionaries, *Distinto amanecer* portrays the failure of the Mexican Revolution to provide real social and economic change for a large segment of the population.

Salón México (originally titled *Mujer mala*, evil woman), Fernández's first film set in the post–World War II period, also dramatizes the conflicted position of women in the economic and social sphere. Like *Distinto amanecer*, this film is concerned with women as desiring subjects.[2] Repeating the plot of *Las abandonadas*, Mercedes (Marga López) in *Salón México* is a dance-hall hostess secretly supporting the education of her sister, Beatriz, at a private boarding school. Mercedes also supports her pimp, Paco (Rodolfo Acosta), a physically and emotionally abusive small-time thief. Like many of Fernandez's films, *Salón México* polarizes moral and social issues and reflects these oppositions through the film's characters. Although poverty, violence against women, and racial inequalities are portrayed in the film, the ideological basis of this abuse is ignored.

The Mexican cabaretera cinema of the 1940s and 1950s, which on the surface struggled to present a sympathetic portrait of working women, remained as conflicted as the earlier narratives. The films maintained the conventional divisions between public and private spheres and male and female social positions, at the same time justifying the dance-hall hostesses' "chosen" profession. The figure of the working woman in the cabaretera was forced to embody traditional notions of womanhood and sacrifice while sustaining a revised form of patriarchy.

However, this new patriarchy was as riddled with contradictions as previous forms. Ramirez Berg, writing of a later manifestation of the genre, suggests that while the cabaretera films of the 1970s do objectify women, "what they mostly do is reveal the desperate state of patriarchy in crisis" (1992a, 125). As will be seen, the cabaretera films of the 1940s reflect a similar crisis of ideology.

Distinto amanecer

Distinto amanecer begins as a classical espionage thriller. In fact, references to the cabaretera do not emerge until halfway through the film, and there is only one extended scene that actually takes place in the Tabu, the dance hall where Julieta works. Why, then, do I include this film in the category of the cabaretera? Many critics of Mexican films in fact do not incorporate Distinto amanecer into their discussion of the cabaret genre. Mora, for example, situates the beginnings of this genre in the era of President Alemán's administration. However, as I suggest above, the time frame of the genre was much more fluid. Bracho's film emerged during a transitional moment when both the industry and the nation were moving from the progressive era of Cárdenas' presidency into the more conservative administration of Ávila Camacho. But more important, Distinto amanecer may be classified as part of the cabaretera genre because the central protagonist is a woman who has been forced into the cabaret by economic necessity and who must come to terms with the complex social demands patriarchy imposed upon Mexican women in the 1940s.

The opening title montage, a series of unconnected shots depicting Octavio being chased by an unidentified man, initially positions Octavio as the protagonist of the film. Falsely implicated in the assassination of a labor union rival by government officials who are trying to cover up widespread corruption, he slips into a movie theater to hide from men who have been hired to kill him.[3] Though Octavio appears to be the central character, a second narrative strand that emerges in the first scene suggests Julieta will play a pivotal role in the film.

In the movie theater, Octavio unknowingly sits next to Julieta, a former girlfriend. As Julieta strikes a match to light a cigarette, Octavio immediately blows it out, fearing that the light will attract the attention of the men pursuing him. Julieta angrily asks him, "What right do you have to do that?" Here, she appears to represent the "new" Mexican woman by questioning the man's privilege to order her around. Octavio points to a "No Smoking" sign to justify his position. However, Julieta strikes another match and points to a sign that advertises "Smoke a Monte Carlo." She again reacts to what she perceives as Octavio's attempt to deny her pleasure and, at the same time, asserts her right to do as she pleases.

While it is true that by 1943 women in Mexico had acquired certain economic rights — the right to work for low wages and to consume expensive products — as noted earlier, these rights did not yet extend to the social or political realm. Thus, just as the Revolution offered lower-class men the privilege of machismo to take the place of real social and economic changes, so too were women given new liberties — the freedom to get a job as a dance-hall hostess and to smoke in public — while being denied access to more important political freedoms.

Once they recognize each other, Julieta invites Octavio home. She and her husband, Ignacio, agree to help Octavio retrieve from a post office box politically sensitive documents that contain evidence incriminating high-ranking government officials. Julieta, unhappy in her marriage, soon realizes she is still in love with Octavio. When Octavio asks her to flee the city with him the following morning, she must decide whether to go with him or remain with Ignacio. The film thus appears to offer the woman a choice; however, within the limits of the classical Mexican film narrative and the ideological discourses regarding woman's position in postrevolutionary Mexico, Julieta's choice is narrowly circumscribed. In the 1940s, poor women, even those who were married, had no viable alternatives to the home, the brothel, the nightclub, or the convent.

Having women like Julieta working to support their families threatened traditional patriarchy, which privileged the social, sexual, political, and economic superiority of men. Before this change in socioeconomic practice, men used their role as the breadwinner to justify unquestioning submission from women. Now that women were earning a living, and at times a better living than the men, the social position of the male was strongly challenged. In addition, by positioning female characters as "dance-hall hostesses" or prostitutes, film narratives were able to rationalize prostitution and at the same time punish women for disrupting social relations.

Ignacio occupies a traditionally feminized position in the narrative, a condition the film attributes partially to Julieta's role as the family's major economic support and partially to the failure of the state to ensure men's superior status. He is initially portrayed as a powerless and weak individual who is unable to care properly for his family or produce a son. Ignacio blames his lack of work on failed economic policies, but the social and economic forces that drove Julieta into working in a cabaret are not explored.[4] Moreover, while women like Julieta were maligned because of their relationship to economic production as sexual objects and to the economy of reproduction as barren (and therefore disgraced) wives, Ignacio's reproductive capabilities are never overtly questioned. This is due to the ideology of machismo, which emphasizes men's virility as a defining and legitimizing characteristic of male power.

Once a part of the intellectual revolutionary movement advocating social and economic justice for all sectors of Mexican society, Ignacio now complains bitterly that "we live in a country where the government has ruined everything. A taxi driver earns more than a teacher." His disaffection from the government places him in a precarious position. As Ramirez Berg defines it, Mexican machismo "is the name of the mutual agreement between the patriarchal state and the individual male in Mexico" (1992a, 107). Because of this ideological link between males and the state, men like Ignacio feel especially betrayed. However, since they cannot, in patriotic conscience, retaliate against the nation, their suppressed anger is taken out on women, whose changing social status threatens them even more.

Ignacio's lack of sufficient employment has forced Julieta to take a degrading job as a cabaret hostess, thus challenging his remaining position of authority as head of the family (according to Mexican machismo). To make matters worse, Julieta has failed to produce a son, further undermining his masculinity. In retaliation for what he perceives to be his demasculinization, he has taken a mistress, another woman whose economic survival is also contingent on limited choices. Ignacio has one woman out in the marketplace and another at home, where she belongs. Interestingly, neither woman seems to fit the classical La Malinche/Virgin of Guadalupe paradigm. The mistress betrays the nation through her illicit relationship with a married man, although she functions as the "good woman" by staying at home. Julieta is the legal wife, but her job in the cabaret positions her as the "bad woman." In social discourse, and in the particular narrative of *Distinto amanecer,* the two proscribed positions for women are antithetical: they cannot be occupied by the same character, thus demonstrating machismo's either/or narrative categorization of woman.

Initially, it appears that the film will be about the need for Octavio to retrieve the documents and get out of town on the 8 o'clock train the following morning. Various events in the film work toward either hindering or furthering the success of his mission. The fact that the story takes place within a twenty-four-hour period and that there are constant references to his deadline reinforce the urgency of the resolution of this plot. However, a second story soon surfaces and works to create a tension between male and female subjectivity. E. Ann Kaplan notes a corresponding sexual dialectic at work in Fritz Lang's *Blue Gardenia,* which, she argues, demonstrates "two modes of articulating a vision of reality" (1980, 83). In a similar way, the double narrative point of view of *Distinto amanecer* juxtaposes male and female perspectives.

While the film relates Octavio's narrative in a classical linear fashion, moving him steadily toward his goal, Julieta's story is not so straightforward. Her narrative, focused on more personal and private issues, subverts the conventions of the classical masculine narrative by momentarily stopping the forward movement of the man's story. While López suggests that the female protagonists of the cabaretera films threaten classical narrative resolution through an "excess of signification," in this case the threat also unfolds as an "excess of structuration" as Julieta's story interrupts and thus forestalls narrative closure (1991a, 44).

As noted, on one level *Distinto amanecer* can be read as a male thriller, complete with government spies, murder, and a ticking clock. On another level, however, it resembles the classic woman's melodrama. Such hybridizations are symptomatic of the fluidity of Mexican genres in the 1940s. Although the plot is structured as a male narrative and it is Octavio's goal that begins the story, the woman surfaces at certain moments in the narrative, and it is a female subjectivity that appears to structure the film's final resolution. Toward the end of the film there is a scene in which this structural tension is explicitly revealed.

Julieta returns to the hotel room where Octavio is hiding. He has the documents in his possession and there is nothing preventing his escape, the conclusion toward which the film has been moving. However, Julieta's narrative has been circling around another closure dependent on her decision to leave with Octavio or stay with her husband.

Tired, Julieta falls asleep in a chair. A slow dissolve to a montage of scenes of the city at sunrise (the first intrusion of daylight into the film) denotes the passage of time. The last shot in the montage is of the train station, and it is marked by the sound of the train's whistle, signaling both its imminent departure and narrative closure. Back in the hotel room, Julieta is awakened by the whistle and tells Octavio about her dream.

Julieta occupies multiple positions in this scene. She is both the dreamer and the subject of the dream. The camera focuses on her and dollies in to a medium close-up, remaining fixed on her while she narrates her dream. There are no cutaways to show Octavio listening. While the dream is marginal to the narrative advancement of Octavio's goals, it works to interrupt the forward development of his story. If the function of woman in this scene is to delay the closure of the male's narrative, at the same time (in relation to Julieta's story) the dream foregrounds another possible narrative ending.

In the dream, Julieta and Octavio are walking through the city while waiting for the train that will take them away. A bell rings, causing Julieta to lose consciousness *within the dream*. She says, "I returned to reality [within the dream] and you weren't you. I started to run as the train's windows sped by me. It gained speed as though it were a runaway train. Then, I opened my eyes and saw the window illuminated by the morning light."

Julieta's dream contains multiple planes of reality, all at odds with one another. On the first level, Julieta, as object, is waiting (a passive position often assigned to women in classical narrative structures) for Octavio (the "active" subject) to take her away. Then Julieta awakens to another level and the realization that Octavio is not who she thinks he is (the subject of her "dreams"). Finally, on yet a third level, Julieta returns to another reality — and the possibility of un distinto amanecer.

Though Julieta's dream momentarily delays the forward movement of the male plot, it is Octavio's goal and the train's departure that finally move the narrative to its conclusion. As Annette Kuhn notes, when female sexuality and female discourse threaten the coherence of the classic narrative, the "threat must be recuperated or repressed if the story is to have any kind of 'satisfactory' resolution—a closure, that is, in which most or all the ends of the narrative are tied up" (1982, 104). Julieta's story poses a threat to the classical narrative in the same way that female sexuality, discourse, and power in the economic and social sphere posed a threat to Mexican machismo and Mexican patriarchy.

Julieta decides to go off with Octavio, but first she must return to her apartment to say goodbye to Ignacio and Juanito. Octavio, afraid she will change her mind, gives her the documents in order to ensure her return. He is afraid he will "lose her a second time" to Ignacio. Julieta promises him she will be at the station at eight.

As Julieta descends the dark staircase of the hotel, she passes (and ignores) a woman on her hands and knees, washing the floor. Doubly oppressed as both a woman and a member of the lower class of the urban indigenous population, this woman has not been given the opportunity to awaken to a new morning. She has not been granted the limited economic and social access that women of Julieta's class have achieved.[5] This moment hints at yet another narrative strand that is never explicitly pursued in the film, which has to do with class differences between women.

The scene then dissolves into a shot of Julieta, dressed in a black evening gown, emerging into the light and walking down the middle of the street against the oncoming traffic, that focuses on the woman in a fairly traditional melodramatic way. This shot, following the scene that privileges Julieta's moment of subjectivity, reemphasizes the possibility of the narrative expression of a female desire.

When Julieta arrives back at her apartment, she finds a letter from Ignacio admitting to his infidelity and failures and releasing her from any commitment to their marriage. It seems that it is too little, too late, however. At eight o'clock, Julieta stands next to Octavio on the train. She hands Ignacio's letter to Octavio, and as he reads it, we hear Ignacio's words: "I hope you find the happiness I couldn't give you." Octavio tears the letter up, and the film cuts to a close-up of Julieta.

"I'd like to know what you're thinking," Octavio says in a voice-off.

Although she does not answer, the camera remains on Julieta, and the spectator is allowed access to her thoughts through her voice-over.

Again Octavio's narrative is momentarily obstructed as Julieta explores the nonlinear structure of her memory.

"Where are you going?" Juanito's voice-over asks.

"I'd like to hold on to you," Ignacio's voice reiterates.

Finally, Julieta remembers Octavio's words in the hotel room: "I don't want to lose you a second time."

Julieta's own voice emerges: "I am at a crossroad; one for love and the other for duty. I don't know which of them will split me in half." The film's ending is thus positioned as Julieta's choice between love for a man who is not her husband and duty to her family, a choice she has been working toward since Octavio sat down next to her in the cinema. It seems that no other possibilities are available to her. She has not been offered the choice to leave the cabaretera; she does not even consider choosing neither man and going off on her own, for such a choice was not readily available to Mexican women in the 1940s.

Julieta's dream may be seen as foreshadowing the film's ending. As she awakens to the reality of her life, she awakens also to the possibility of love and passion and an escape from a dismal existence. However, the dream could be referring to the realization that Octavio is not who she thinks he is. In the end, the narrative recuperates female subjectivity by suggesting that the choice Julieta ultimately makes is one that will open up new possibilities and will provide un distinto amanecer for all of Mexico's women. And because the ending is presented as one that is chosen, Julieta is made available as a positive role model for women sitting in Mexico's darkened cinemas.

As the train pulls away, Julieta is revealed standing by the tracks with Juanito as Ignacio approaches. When Juanito asks why she's crying, she replies, "I would have cried even more if I'd left." Though Julieta chooses to remain with her family, it is not clear whether she makes this choice out of love or duty. Similarly, it is unclear whether Julieta is actually able to chart her own destiny, since both the parameters of her choice and the meaning of the "new morning" are circumscribed by sexual and narrative discourses. Moreover, as Kaplan observes in regard to Hollywood films, the intercession of the thriller genre finally "legitimizes the ultimate control of the narrative by a male protagonist" (1990, 135).

The family walks away together as the final words of a popular song promise *un distinto amanecer para las mujeres* (a new morning for women). But what, specifically, will be different, and for which women? Will women's choices be continuously limited to choosing between two men? Will all women eventually have the choice *not* to be dance-hall hostesses or prostitutes? Judith Mayne reads a similarly contradictory ending in the Soviet film *Fragment of an Empire* as "a sign of incoherence, incoherence in the sense that many of the issues raised in the film cannot be wrapped up neatly in a narrative conclusion" (1989, 153).

The conventions of the classical Mexican narrative and postrevolutionary patriarchy demanded narrative and feminine containment. Julieta's initial decision to leave Ignacio is articulated outside the boundaries of "his" story and thus cannot easily be incorporated into the dominant narrative of Mexican cinema or society. However, at the same time, narrative closure cannot finally contain all the expressions of feminine desire or satisfy all social conflicts. The film's ending thus evokes ambiguity rather than melodramatic pleasure in the nobility of woman's sacrifice. As López argues, even if Mexican melodramas ultimately failed to produce a female subjectivity, they did manage to "mediate the crisis of national and gendered identity . . . [by staging] specific dramas of identity which often complicated straightforward ideological identification for men and women without precluding accommodation" (1991a, 36).

Salón México

Like Julieta, Mercedes in *Salón México* articulates what Jorge Ayalo Blanco calls the central theme of the cabaretera genre: "the double life" of women in this period of economic instability (1968, 164). The film mirrors this theme visually and conceptually through the alternation between darkness and light, good and evil, and mother and whore. The world of the cabaret with its smoky dance halls, its dark and shabby hotels with unlit staircases and broken windows, is transformed with a mere cinematic dissolve to the brightly lit rooms of the College for Young Women, where cigarette smoke, alcohol, and prostitution cannot intrude.

The main character, Mercedes, must stoop to the lowest depths to provide for her family. She maintains two distinct lives: one in the caba-

Figure 4.4. Mercedes (María Félix) articulates what Ayalo Blanco calls the central theme of the cabaretera genre: "the double life" of women in this period of economic instability. *Salón México*, production still.

ret milieu of the night, as an object of men's desires and whims, the other as the good mother who works six days a week, sacrificing her own life for her sister's. In this way, Fernández's film offers up a moral excuse for prostitution rather than a socioeconomic one. At the same time, however, Mercedes must be punished for trespassing the boundaries of what is considered acceptable womanly behavior, although her transgression is ultimately rationalized as a personal sacrifice for the future of Mexico and the Mexican family. The film's narrative turns on the conflict between Mercedes' need for money and her desire to keep her profession a secret from her young sister, Beatriz. The opening scene of the film sets up this conflict but does not reveal its foundation, and thus Mercedes at first appears to be a "bad" woman whose only ambition is to accumulate money.

Fernández and Figueroa adapted the cinematic techniques they developed in their earlier films to *Salón México*, but instead of rural land-scapes and maguey plants, they filmed the new urbanscapes: museums, government buildings, and tenements. The film opens with one of these urban images: an exterior, low-angle shot looking up at a neon sign flashing off and on, inviting customers into the Salón México. The camera follows men and women into the crowded, smoke-filled nightclub.[6] A few couples are dancing, but it is soon obvious they did not come in together. It is mostly men who sit at the tables—drinking, smoking and talking—while the women silently line the walls, waiting for a paying customer.

Unlike *Distinto amanecer*, the cabaretera theme is revealed immedi-ately in *Salón México*. A danzón contest is announced, and Mercedes and Paco, couple number 3, are identified as the favorites. After they win, Paco refuses to give up Mercedes' share of the prize money—fifty pesos—no matter how much she begs him. Handing her a cheap trophy instead, he leaves the dance hall with another woman. Desper-ate, Mercedes steals the money from Paco's pocket while he sleeps. A policeman named Lupe sees Mercedes toss the empty wallet on the street outside the hotel. The theft of what is rightfully hers eventually leads to Mercedes' punishment, not at the hands of the law, repre-sented by Lupe, but by Paco, who represents the law of machismo.

Mercedes is the whore with the virgin's heart of gold, sacrificing herself, as any mother should, for the good of her family. Though Paco abuses her physically and emotionally, she remains dependent on him for her livelihood; so much for the economic liberation of women in postrevolutionary Mexican society.

When Mercedes goes to meet her sister for their customary Sunday visit, she dresses in a tailored suit, hat, and sensible shoes, having dis-carded the spike heels of the previous night. This respectable outfit is not enough for the director of the school, however, who warns Mer-cedes that she needs to spend more time with Beatriz. Mercedes tries to explain that she must work long hours and do much traveling, which prevents her from being with her sister as much as she would like to be. The director, even though she is also a working woman, seems not to understand the multiple demands imposed on lower-class women, who must function as mother, father, and financial support for their families.

As Mercedes and Beatriz exit the gates of the college, they are confronted by Lupe. Understanding the situation at once, Lupe does not bring up the matter of the theft or the cabaret. By virtue of her sacrifice, Mercedes is redeemed in his eyes, both in terms of her crime and in terms of her work as one of Paco's girls. Lupe immediately falls in love with her and takes it upon himself, as a man and as a public servant, to rescue her from Paco and from prostitution. He thus represents, as I will show later, another, more benevolent side of machismo.

Though Fernández's film treats Mercedes' position with compassion, it is not an endorsement of female sexuality or even a call to reform sexual mores. However, *Salón México* promises that mothers, and mother figures like Mercedes, who sacrifice their lives for the benefit of young girls like Beatriz—the idealized virgin, cloistered in a school with other young women of the upper class—will be rewarded with the respect traditionally reserved for martyrs.

Called on to deliver a speech in class, Beatriz chooses heroism as her topic. In addition to such well-known heroes as St. Francis and St. Bernard, Louis Pasteur and Madame Curie, and the military men who "defend our families . . . risking their lives on land, sea, and in the skies," Beatriz argues that heroism, as personal sacrifice, "can be found hidden in the dark recesses of a mother's heart when she heroically overcomes misery and passionately tries to give her child the world." Unknowingly, Beatriz has described her sister's role, although throughout the film the young girl fails to understand Mercedes' absence from her daily life. Sacrifice, in this film, is inscribed as the supreme virtue of mothering. In this way, the La Malinche/whore figure may be redeemed as a mother who gave up her own freedom for the future of her sons and daughters.

Beatriz fulfills the role of the virgin in *Salón México*. Not only is she innocent sexually, but she is also not aware of the work her sister does so that she can be educated as an upper-class girl. However, while the Virgin of Guadalupe represented a fusion of national and ethnic differences, Beatriz represents the fusion of classes in Fernández's film, enacting for the audience the future of womanhood in Mexico. Through her marriage to Roberto, an upper-class criollo, who is the son of the school's director, Beatriz will contribute to the blurring of class difference, a requirement of nationalistic ideology in the 1940s that sought to create a new sense of cultural unity.

Early in the film, Beatriz informs Mercedes that she has fallen in love with, and wants to marry, Roberto. When Mercedes realizes that her sister will be taken care of financially and emotionally, she agrees to Lupe's entreaties that she give up her work and marry him. However, one night Paco surprises her in her room and threatens to blackmail her if she does not accompany him to Guatemala after a bungled robbery attempt. Afraid that if her secret is revealed, Beatriz's chance to ascend into the upper class will be jeopardized, Mercedes stabs Paco repeatedly with a knife. Before he dies, he pulls out his gun and shoots her. The next morning Roberto and Lupe go to the morgue together to claim her body. Lupe protects her terrible secret, even in death, telling Roberto only that Mercedes was going to be his wife. "She was," he informs him, "the greatest woman I've ever known." Not able to recover her status as a good woman in life, Mercedes is redeemed through death by the graces of a good man.

Masculinity and Femininity

It is telling that in both *Salón México* and *Distinto amanecer* biological reproduction is absent. Neither Mercedes nor Julieta can be defined as female by virtue of having given birth, though they are aligned with the duties and functions of motherhood. This absence, however, signifies something more than biological dysfunction; it points to social fears regarding the collapse of the traditional Mexican family due to transformations in woman's social and economic role.

While changes in the family occurred in response to the effects of economic and social pressures of poverty, migration, and the increasingly paternal role of the state, on a narrative and cinematic level the blame is transferred to women. In neither film are the social forces that spawn prostitution addressed. It is women's economic role—tied to an aggressive, visible, and barren sexuality—that threatens the position of the male and the stability of the family in postrevolutionary Mexican society. If woman (and woman's position as subservient to men) is defined in part by the ability to give birth, then the *inability* to reproduce signifies (for patriarchy) either that the subject is not a woman or that she is in violation of patriarchal law. According to the logic of patriarchy, it could never denote a failure of male productive power,

Figure 4.5. As their family disintegrates, Julieta (Andrea Palma) attempts to offer consolation to her young brother. In many of the films of the 1940s, the blame for the collapse of the moral fabric of the traditional way of life is laid upon the backs of women. *Distinto amanecer,* production still.

Figure 4.6. Roberto, the military man, and Lupe, the policeman, offer Mexican audiences examples of the "good" side of machismo: men who will lay down their lives for their nation. *Salón México*, production still.

either sexual or social. This failure lies at the center of *Salón México* and is specifically symbolized through representations of different forms of machismo.

The cabaretera films of this era expressed an ideological indictment of both the negative sexual aspects of machismo and the paternal authority of the state. As outlined earlier, Mexican machismo provided a "link between male and state," awarding each with reciprocal support and allegiance (Ramirez Berg, 1989, 171). If, as suggested before, the Mexican state was experiencing a "crisis of patriarchy," then this crisis could also be read as a crisis of masculinity on the individual or psychological level. In addition to the conflicted representation of women's roles, this male crisis also emerges in the cabaretera narratives.

In *Salón México*, for instance, a number of different categories of maleness and machismo are defined not only by the obvious code of dress that marks social class, but also by mannerisms, speech, and action. Paco signifies one type of Mexican macho, the *pachuco*, a lower-class, uneducated male caught in a kind of perpetual adolescence who, lacking real social power, relies on his sexual virility to reconfirm his position in society. He wears flashy American clothing, exploits women for a living, and resorts to violence to achieve his goals. He functions as a representation of the traditional and negative aspects of Mexican machismo wherein violence and force were regularly employed.

Before the dance contest in the opening scene, Paco warns the judges that he must win: "Whoever doesn't vote for me, get rid of them." When Mercedes begs him for her share of the money, he responds, "Don't bother me anymore, or I'll clobber you right here on the street!" And as he's beating Mercedes in the hotel room, Paco warns her to give him the money she took from him, "or I'll kick you to death." It is in this representation of negative male power that the movie offers its strongest indictment of Mexican patriarchy. The pachuco represents all that is wrong with Mexico: the lower-class male's rejection of his indigenous roots, his adoption of foreign dress and mannerisms (specifically those of the United States), and his penchant for violence.

Conversely, Lupe, the policeman, characterizes another side of machismo, a side that Ramirez Berg defines as "humane, responsible, and protective" (1992a, 23). Lupe is identified as a man of Indian ancestry who insists that he is nothing more than a "son of the people," even though his uniform indicates that he represents the Law. He is strong, yet subservient when relating to the authority of the upper class. He is completely moral. And he places the welfare of the nation above his own life.

However, it is a third category of the male, portrayed by the soldier Roberto, who signifies the future of male power in Mexico. Roberto, a well-educated criollo, stands in as a metonymic symbol of the Mexican state. According to patriarchal ideology, the postrevolutionary social and economic crisis would be overcome when males were restored their "natural" rights and positions of power. Roberto symbolizes this idealized position. In addition to being white and a member of the upper class, he is a national hero, and, more important, he was wounded and was awarded medals by the United States. He is assertive but polite with women and with racial and class inferiors. When Lupe brings him information about a meeting with Mercedes, Roberto generously hands the policeman a tip for his work. Later, Lupe tells Mercedes that Roberto "sparkles of importance. He gave me two pesos as a tip and I think I'll keep them as mementos." For Lupe, the lower-class workingman who makes only six pesos a month, Roberto is the symbol of both the authority and the benevolence of the state.

This film dramatizes the conflicting discourse surrounding machismo and reveals how ideology veils such conflicts. Although machismo emerged in different forms in Mexico and served in all forms to suppress women, it also functioned to confirm the logic of class and ethnic difference, because certain men, the upper-class males of European ancestry, enjoyed social and economic privileges denied to lower-class mestizos and Indian men.

Space and Sexual Difference

In her discussion of the eighteenth-century novel and Hollywood film melodramas of the 1940s, Judith Mayne locates three areas that define socially and narratively gendered spaces: "the economic organization of production, the family, and the definition of male and female roles." In Hollywood cinema, the difference between public and private spheres was often visibly traced through the relation between gender and space. In these melodramas, men were linked with the public sphere—politics, commerce, and the law—while women were generally aligned with the private domain of domesticity. However, Mayne points out that not only are these relations at base ideological, but also, in reality, "the boundaries between private and public space are not always as clearly marked" between male and female (1988, 19).

Similarly, in the Mexican cabaretera melodrama, the division between public and private is not easily distinguishable on the basis of male versus female, even on an ideological level. In the cabaretera films, woman acts as a disruption in the home, at work, and in the various sites that signify the nation. For example, if the cabaretera was defined as a public space of production wherein women sold their bodies to men, it also functioned as a private sphere in which women were able to form social and personal relationships with each other, relationships that excluded men. Likewise, while the home traditionally served as a place where a woman could exert her rights as wife and mother, in these films it no longer functions as the site of refuge it once was.

Dana Polan notes that representations of traditional cinematic spaces of safety in the Hollywood films of the 1940s (such as the home and the small town) came to symbolize an "instability." Conversely, the city, once a place of crime and violence (for example in the early gangster films of the 1930s), functioned in the 1940s "as a place of ultimate ambiguity . . . a plethora of narrative possibilities," a locus of uncertainty (1986, 234–236). In *Distinto amanecer, Salón México,* and other cabaretera films, representations of public places also were filled with ambiguous meaning: while on one hand the city symbolized a potential danger, on the other hand it offered the possibility of community, pleasure, and profit. As García Riera puts it, *Salón México* presents an ambiguous vision of "a Mexico that should not be" and, at the same time, "a Mexico that should be" (1963, 307).

In these films, the dance hall exemplified a microcosm of the city, with its multiplicity of ethnicities, classes, and expressions of sexuality. Moreover, it was the cabaretera, not the home, that offered a margin of freedom for women like Julieta and Mercedes. In an increasingly industrialized urban environment, with high unemployment and increasing poverty, the home in Mexico ceased to serve as a place of refuge for women of the lower classes, while places like the cabaret provided at least a modicum of opportunity.

Women in the more privileged echelons of society, although oppressed by patriarchal and class restrictions, were still protected from poverty and random violence by virtue of their families' social status, wealth, and advantage. In describing the opening of the 1941 film *Cuando los hijos se van* (Juan Bustillo Oro), Ramirez Berg writes that a "long shot of the outer walls and gates" of a middle-class family home defines "the borders between public and private" (1992a, 17–18). However, while the middle and upper classes, locked behind the safety of high stone walls and relative economic security, could claim an exclusive and secure privacy, this was generally not available to the majority of Mexico's population, of which Mercedes and Julieta were a part.

Mercedes' home at first seems to offer a retreat from the exterior world of the dance hall. Here, in the secrecy of her one-room flat, she can transform herself from a prostitute into a respectable working woman. However, her home turns out to be a dangerous space that the male can forcibly enter without even paying for the woman's services, and it ultimately is the space in which her life is destroyed. Similarly, Julieta's home exposes her to danger from a male intruder, and, like Mercedes, she is forced to kill, in self-defense, a man who intrudes into the space of her home.

Certain urban spaces are privileged as the site of the "public" in both *Distinto amanecer* and *Salón México*. Parks, museums, cinemas, and city streets are meant to signify the space of national identity. In these locations, individuals of various classes, races, and genders merge to become "the people." In *Salón México*, public sites that are already imbued with national significance are used as backdrops for the narrative in order to foreground Fernández's primary intention: the production of a specifically Mexican national cinema.

Fernández appropriated both Mexican pre-Columbian and contemporary art to construct his portraits of *mexicanidad*. On a Sunday outing with Beatriz, Mercedes takes her to the National Museum of Anthropology. The scene opens on the face of an immense pre-Columbian stone effigy. In a trademark Fernández/Figueroa low-angle shot, Mercedes and Beatriz are framed against the backdrop of this ancient face in an attempt to link the past to the present and to endow woman with a connection to Fernández's imagined notion of a Mexican national identity.

This connection is also made evident in the scene immediately following, when, later that evening, Mercedes and Beatriz join with thousands of other Mexicans in the streets below the Palacio Nacional on Independence Day in 1942 to celebrate President Camacho's commitment to support, in spirit at least, the Allied forces in their war against fascism (although Mexico had no significant role in World War II). Waving tiny Mexican flags, the two women, surrounded by their compatriots, shout "Viva México! Viva México!" National pride is proclaimed as all-encompassing in the forum of the city's streets, which are presented as a boundless area where people may gather to work, play, and celebrate their relations as Mexicans while divisions of race, class, and sexual difference are effaced in the celebration of a shared national history.

The Other Woman

While feminists have been concerned with how Woman has been defined as Other in relation to man, it is necessary also to consider how women are opposed to *each other* in terms of class, race, and ethnic difference. In *Distinto amanecer*, both Julieta and Ignacio's mistress are presented as whores: Julieta by virtue of her work, the mistress because she is not the "legal" wife. Julieta emerges as the "good" woman at the end of the film because, under patriarchy, she occupies the socially sanctioned position and because her work is considered productive in the economic sphere. The "other" woman, however, produces nothing that is valued in society, threatens the primacy of the family and the sanctity of marriage, and flaunts her sexuality. The mistress is thus identified as the "bad" woman. When Ignacio leaves her (and it is obvious that he will not return), the narrative abandons her as well.

While class and economic function are privileged as a boundary of difference in *Distinto amanecer*, it is race that most visibly defines female difference in cinema. Commenting on Hollywood, Tania Modleski has noted that "if the white woman has usually served as the signifier of male desire, . . . the black woman, when present at all, has served as a signifier of (white) female sexuality" (1991, 128).

Although Mexico does not share a history of slavery with the United States and with other Latin American nations such as Cuba and Brazil, skin color as a mark of difference has permeated Mexican culture since the first mestizos, fathered by white Spanish conquerors, were born to Indian women. Issues of race are central to Mexican history and have been dramatized in Mexican narratives since the colonial period. Like earlier novels and theatrical presentations, the cabaretera investigates this other kind of constructed opposition based on skin color and ancestry.

Some would argue that because women can recognize themselves in other women, they can therefore see beneath the veneer of representation. However, this argument assumes that all women speak and understand the same symbolic language. Moreover, it does not allow for differences of race, class, and social experience in the production of language (and thus of meaning) even within national borders. As Ella Shohat puts it, feminist film theory needs to incorporate the cultural critiques of postcolonial criticism in order to "explore and problematize the implications of these differences [among women] for the representation of gender relations within racially and culturally non-homogeneous textual environments" (1991, 45).

Many Chicana feminists are examining race in regard to the representation of the mestiza in Chicano and Mexican films.[7] Carmen Huaco-Nuzum points out, for instance, that classical Mexican films often used white actresses to portray indigenous and mestiza women, thereby glossing over ethnic differences and creating monolithic stereotypes of Mexican women (1992, 129). In both *Distinto amanecer* and *Salón México*, notions of racial otherness emerged as expressions of female sexuality that surfaced on the bodies of Afro-Cuban women performing the erotically suggestive rumbas and mambos. The representation of these "exotic" women and their musical performances resisted the narrative containment of the classical devices of Mexican cinema.

López rightly categorizes the musical excesses of the cabaretera as representing the flip side of repressed female sexuality, writing that "the exotic rumbera was a social fantasy through which other subjectivities could be envisioned, other psychosexual/social identities forged" (1991a, 46). Primarily, this was because in the historical context of these films, the fantasies were imported and could not be mistaken for Mexican. However, there is a split between the performance of the danzón by lighter-skinned mestizo women and the performance of the rumba by those with darker skins, and thus between what kinds of expressions of desire and pleasure Mercedes and Julieta are allowed, and the kinds of desires these Other women give voice to.

In *Salón México*, although the performances of the rumba by dark-skinned women are separated and distinguished from the main narrative, they still serve as transition devices in the overall strategy of the film's thematic design. At the same time, operating outside the primary narrative framework, representations of black women also force an acknowledgment of the relation of otherness and distance between women based on skin color.

At the conclusion of the dance contest in *Salón México*, there is a cut from a wide shot of Mercedes chasing after Paco back into the interior of the dance hall, where a group of dark-skinned dancers are performing a rumba. While the scene abruptly disturbs the central conflict between Paco and Mercedes, there is an ideological connection between the narrative and the performance. The intrusion of the rumba inserts alternative expressions of desire that were not available for Mexican women. The performance by a group of dark-skinned Afro-Cuban women represents what cannot be represented by Mercedes and other mestizo and light-skinned Mexican women. Mercedes is confined to the danzón, where motion and emotion are repressed and female sexuality is obscured by slow, stylized, and male-controlled movements.

These musical interludes may be considered as instances of narrative resistance responding to the contradictions and struggles operating within Mexican postrevolutionary social discourses. The melodramatic excess that emerges at these moments of performance functions as a response to sexual and social repression based on gender and on race.

As discussed previously, La Malinche was an ambiguous figure, serving both as Mexico's version of Eve—the mother of modern Mexico—and as a national traitor. While the female cabaretera figures reproduce the dichotomy of mother/whore, at the same time the cabaretera films offer a terrain for analyzing moments in which this enigmatic signification breaks down. The classical Mexican narrative could not successfully represent a female figure who embodied this ideological dichotomy, and thus there were moments in which these dance-hall films offered up a female character with whom Mexican women could identify in their shared experience of social and economic oppression. As Linda Williams suggests, "it does not take a radical and consciously feminist break with patriarchal ideology to represent the contradictory aspects of the woman's position under patriarchy" (1984, 21).

At the same time, while the cinema of the cabaretera may have suggested the possibility of portraying female desire and subjectivity, the melodramatic narrative ultimately worked to confirm patriarchy, however unstable that structure proved to be. But if the representation of women in the cabaretera films did not succeed in challenging narrative containment, it did provide a space in which female spectators could question narrative and social structures that placed women in the ambiguous position of good woman *and* whore. Although the position of woman in Mexican social and cinematic narratives could not be reshaped until the myth of patriarchy was rewritten, moments in which female desire and female subjectivity erupted to impede narrative resolution reveal both the impossibility of complete containment of woman and the possibility of un distinto amanecer.

5

LA DEVORADORA:

THE MEXICAN FEMME FATALE

Madness, for Buñuel, lies always in characters whose surroundings
and ideals are based on beliefs and traditional morality.
Max Lautenegge and Mario Gerteis

The figure of the femme fatale recurs in numerous mythological, literary, and cinematic traditions. Although the particular representation
of this powerful female archetype changes in response to historical
and psychic mechanisms, the symbolic function of the femme fatale as
a threat to male authority remains constant. Specifically, her perceived
control over life (through procreation) and death (through symbolic
castration) challenges the stability of patriarchal ideology in classical
narrative texts. In order to contain this threat, the femme fatale must
be destroyed or made powerless.

In this chapter, I examine the Mexican version of the femme fatale
in two films: *Doña Bárbara* (Fernando de Fuentes, 1943) and *Susana* (Luis
Buñuel, 1950). Doña Bárbara's threat emerges in the form of a denial
and a repression of female sexuality, whereas the femme fatale in *Susana*
poses other kinds of dangers through her flaunting of femininity.

As a motif defined foremost by sexual difference and sexual excess,
the femme fatale in Hollywood mainstream cinema disrupted narrative and representational continuity by her excessive sexuality. She
was most visible in the postwar film noir cinema as the "black widow"
who entrapped unsuspecting men in her deadly web of deceit. While
woman in the classical Hollywood cinema was often positioned as the
object of the male hero's goals, in film noir, the femme fatale surfaces

as a more conflicted and threatening character, "the dark lady, the spider woman, the evil seductress," in the words of Janey Place (1980, 35).

Mexican cinema produced its own negative female figure, the mala mujer, a reincarnation of the archetypal Terrible Mother that Herrera-Sobek discusses. In early "seduced and abandoned" films like *Santa,* and in the later cabaretera films, such as *Salón México* and *Distinto amanecer,* women may be forced into prostitution due to economic misfortunes, but they remain essentially "good women." However, in other films, such as *La mujer del puerto* (Arcady Boytler, 1933), *Crepúsculo* (Julio Bracho, 1944), *La mujer sin alma* (Fernando de Fuentes, 1943), and *La devoradora* (Fernando de Fuentes, 1946), the female-gone-bad characters are represented as "cruel and vengeful vampires, without sexual scruples, usurping the cruelty of men, enslaving, beautiful, and unfeeling"—la devoradora, the "devouring woman" (Ayala Blanco, 1968, 145). This evil figure, by her very visibility and, at the same time, inscrutability, challenged the fragile coherence of many classical Mexican film narratives.

Mary Ann Doane, in her study of the recurrence of the femme fatale in various traditions and guises, argues that this symbol of the threatening woman materializes as an articulation of male fear about female sexuality. The male protagonist regains control through his desire for her. According to Doane, the femme fatale therefore can be considered only a conduit of male power rather than a source of power in her own right. Although Doane does concede that the femme fatale "is not totally under the control of its producers," she ignores specific challenges posed by this sign of excessive and dangerous femininity. To suggest, as Doane does, that the femme fatale's power "is usually not subject to her will" and that she "is not the subject of power but its *carrier,*" is to deny the real threat that the femme fatale poses to male subjectivity and to narrative coherence (1991, 2).

I would argue, instead, that the very identification of femininity as threatening and the unremitting compulsion to contain such expressions of female power in narrative and in social practice attest to the pervasive force of such power. My interest in this chapter will be to look at moments in the above two films where female power, wielded by la devoradora, emerges (in different ways) to threaten patriarchal ideology in the classical Mexican cinema.

While neither *Susana* nor *Doña Bárbara* is a progressive film in terms of the portrayal of women, they do attest to the way in which expressions of female desire in melodramas may expose and disrupt patriarchal holds on narrative and social representation.

Doña Bárbara

Doña Bárbara, based on a novel by the Venezuelan writer Rómulo Gallegos, stars María Félix as a wronged woman who has discarded the visage of femininity and assumed the privileges of the male. A powerful and wealthy woman who controls hundreds of acres of prime ranch land, numerous head of cattle and horses, and the lives of the men and women who live on her land, Doña Bárbara dresses in men's clothing, takes on the aggressive and paternalistic manners reserved for the Mexican male, and evens rides astride her horse like a man. Because she punishes those who betray her with emotional and physical abuse, and occasionally with death, she is known as "Doña Bárbara, the terrible."[1]

Doña Bárbara opens with a short prologue that distances the story, both spatially and temporally, from 1940s Mexico. Two men sit in the bow of a canoe: a well-dressed young lawyer, Santos Luzardo (Julián Soler), returning to his family home in the outer regions of Venezuela after completing his university studies, and an older man who is guiding the boat up the Orinoco River. To pass the time, the older man relates the story of an earlier journey taken by a young woman who came up this same river "once upon a time." By setting *Doña Bárbara* "in a place and time far from Mexico," the narrative attempts to displace issues of sexuality, class conflicts, and gender relations from Mexican history.[2]

According to the older man, six "brutal men," the captain, and a beautiful young woman made up the crew of a small sailboat traveling up and down the Orinoco River, carrying cargo from port to port. When another man boarded the boat and fell in love with the girl, the jealous crew members killed him and raped the girl. Years later, a woman, Doña Bárbara, appeared on the river in another boat with "rancor in her heart," evil men at her side, and wealth and witchcraft in her trunks. It was the girl, now grown, returning to exact revenge.

From a close-up of Doña Bárbara, the film dissolves forward in time to a shot of a drunken man, Laurencito (Andrés Soler), who turns out to be an old friend of Santos Luzardo and a former lover of Doña Bár-

Figure 5.1. Doña Bárbara (María Félix) is la devoradora, Mexican cinema's
femme fatale. *Doña Bárbara*, production still.

bara's. In a reversal of the usual "seduced and abandoned" stories, Doña Bárbara gave birth to Laurencito's daughter, Marisela, and left the child to be raised by her father. Disgraced and emasculated in the eyes of the local people, Laurencito became an alcoholic, leaving Marisela to grow up on her own, befriended only by Doña Bárbara's half-witted servant. Doña Bárbara thus fulfills the function of the classical femme fatale in this film through her symbolic castration of the father and her abandonment of motherhood. The goal of the narrative is to reinstate the father's potency and power by destroying the efficacy of la devoradora. In addition to reclaiming the land Doña Bárbara has stolen from his family, Santos Luzardo, the film's hero, will need to reclaim the father's power and restore the categories of sexual difference that Doña Bárbara has inverted.

Due to the ambiguity of Doña Bárbara's sexual identity, she is caught in a narrative tangle of contradictions. She consistently refuses the sexual attentions of men because the risk of becoming an object of male desire jeopardizes her self-constructed identity of not-woman. At the same time, she is subject to the ridicule of these men for denying her femaleness and for being neither man nor woman. When she finally discovers in Santos Luzardo a man she desires, patriarchy, which privileges heterosexual relationships, requires that she must first become a woman. However, she cannot accomplish this without giving up those attributes of power which characterize her masculinity, and when she tries out her female identity on Santos Luzardo, she is cruelly rebuked. Ultimately, she must deny her female identity in order to retain her position of authority.

Awaiting Santos Luzardo's arrival to discuss business matters, Doña Bárbara, standing before a mirror, removes her neck scarf, opens the collar of her shirt, lets her hair fall around her shoulders, and admires the image of the woman reflected at her. It is, however, the only desiring response she will receive. When Santos Luzardo experiences her seduction, he refuses to acknowledge her self-constructed female sexuality.

Confronted by this refusal, Doña Bárbara reassumes her masquerade, and when Santos Luzardo presents her with economic and moral ultimatums, she refuses to relinquish her power. Confounded by these contradictions of sexual difference, she resorts to witchcraft to seduce

Figure 5.2. Santos Luzardo (Julián Soler) has returned to his father's home to reclaim his land and the mantle of the patriarch. *Doña Bárbara*, production still.

him. She builds an altar to him, surrounding his framed picture with stars, crosses, and candles. By inverting the picture, she attempts to exert her power over him symbolically. If his power is determined by his maleness, then this inversion in part connotes an antithesis of maleness—or femaleness—in the oppositional structure of the narrative. However, she soon finds that her witchcraft does not work; it is overpowered by the force of an "authentic" masculinity.

Doña Bárbara is ultimately a story about the realignment of the family. The task proves to be a difficult one because, in this film, a family first has to be invented. The parental figures are not really parents in the proper sense: Laurencito trades his daughter for whiskey, and Doña Bárbara has never acknowledged her biological relationship to Marisela. It is Santos Luzardo who finally succeeds in reaffirming the sanctity of the family and the lawful status of the male by assuming the position of the father after Laurencito dies. And, refusing to be tempted by Doña Bárbara's seductive power or by her witchcraft, he annihilates la devoradora.

The daughter, Marisela, through her marriage to the benevolent father figure Santos Luzardo, will complete the construction of the new family by assuming the position of the "good mother." However, this consummation is not accomplished without a struggle. Marisela enters her mother's house, looking for Santos Luzardo. Not finding him there, she proceeds to explore the rooms, searching, perhaps, for evidence of the woman who gave her life but about whom she knows nothing. Marisela spies the altar Doña Bárbara has constructed, and as she moves closer to inspect it, she is startled by the voice of Doña Bárbara asking her what she is looking for. From a close-up of the surprised face of Marisela, the film cuts to a medium shot of her mother leaning against the wall next to a mirror in which Marisela's image is reflected. At this point, the actual figure of the mother dominates the reflected image of the daughter.

"What do you want?" Doña Bárbara repeats.

"The photograph," Marisela answers in a close-up.

Doña Bárbara, asserting her control as a mother, walks toward Marisela in the wider shot. Marisela is again contained in the mirror's frame. "The man belongs to me," Doña Bárbara declares with finality.

The next two-shot finally places the two women on equal terms as Marisela screams *"Bruja!"* (witch) and lunges at her mother. The ensuing fight is broken up by Santos Luzardo. From a two-shot of the women, the film cuts to a medium shot of the man as Marisela crosses into the frame to place herself beside him. The subsequent shot reveals Doña Bárbara standing alone, facing the social and ideological sanctity of the heterosexual couple. Marisela, as a woman, now affirms her authority as Mexican discourse prescribed she could, through her displacement of the maternal figure and her inevitable alignment with the male father.

After Santos Luzardo and Marisela leave, Doña Bárbara hears a voice coming from her empty chair. The voice asks her what she wants, what she is looking for. Turning to her altar, she again inverts Santos Luzardo's picture, then immediately turns it right side up. She understands that her power has been canceled and her desire rejected by its object. Crying, she sits in the chair. "What's happened to me?" she

Figure 5.3. Doña Bárbara and her daughter, Marisela (Maria Elena Marqués), whom she has never acknowledged. In this scene, Marisela will move out from under her mother's power to align herself with the "father," Santos Luzardo. *Doña Bárbara,* production still.

asks. "I can't find myself." Neither woman nor man, she has no identity according to Mexican patriarchal ideology, which recognizes subjects first of all according to sexual difference. In the context of the narrative of the family melodrama, this could be read as a warning to Mexican women to retain their socially defined identity as women or suffer the consequences of nonidentity.

Susana

Susana (released in the United States as *The Devil and the Flesh* and in France as *Susana la perverse*), was based on a work by the Spanish playwright Rodolfo Usigli. Like many of Buñuel's films, it is sustained by the thinnest of plots. The film begins at the State Reformatory for Women during a severe thunderstorm. Susana (Rosita Quintana) is being dragged into an empty cell by three large guards.

In Virginia Higgenbotham's description of the initial incarceration scene, Higgenbotham identifies the guards as male. In fact, they are female, and this relation between Susana and her jailers introduces an important thematic point by establishing that the struggle for power is not limited to differences in gender, race, or economic class, but may occur within these divisions also. This theme is repeated throughout the film in struggles between members of the same class, between men, and between women.

Noticing a shadow in the shape of a cross on the dirt floor of her cell, Susana kneels in front of it and begs the "God of prisoners" to set her free. When a spider, one of Buñuel's recurrent motifs, creeps across the shadow, Susana jumps to the window and rattles the bars. To her surprise, the bars break loose and she climbs out into the storm. Though absurd moments such as these have earned classical Mexican cinema a reputation for being excessively melodramatic ("excessive" in this case being a disparaging label), in Buñuel's Mexican films, they function as a parodic critique of melodrama itself.

Taking refuge at the hacienda of wealthy Don Guadalupe (Fernando Soler) and his wife, Doña Carmen (Matilde Palou), Susana finds temporary freedom and the chance to secure a more permanent social position. Lying about how she came to be out in the storm, she presents herself as an innocent young girl fleeing from the family for whom she worked because the father attempted to rape her.

Recognizing that it is the mother of the household who will make the decision to let her stay, Susana sets about securing Doña Carmen's trust. Then, continuing to spin her web of deception, Susana seduces Don Guadalupe, his son Alberto (Luis López Somoza), and the hacienda foreman, Jesús (Victor Manuel Mendoza)—and betrays the trust and kindness of Doña Carmen, who has offered to be "like a mother" to her. The only character she cannot fool is the family's faithful servant, Perlita, a superstitious woman who believes that Susana is an incarnation of the Devil.

Although the character of Susana is the *object* of desire for the three male characters in the film, she is more importantly a *subject* who desires, and it is these desires that motivate her actions. However, unlike the men, for whom the woman functions as an object of erotic pleasure—apparently beautiful young women provide nothing else— Susana sees men as the means to achieve her goals of wealth, social status, and power.

Buñuel has said that *Susana* is one of his least favorite films, though he does regret "not pushing the caricature of the happy ending" (1983, 202). By the conclusion of the film, Susana has succeeded in seducing all three men and turning them against one another. Alberto has denounced his mother and father, Jesús has betrayed the trust of his employer, and Don Guadalupe has turned against his family, going so far as to order them away from the hacienda so that he may live there with Susana. However, at the last minute, the police arrive. Jesús, overcome with jealousy, has turned Susana in, and in a repetition of the opening scene, Susana is dragged off to be imprisoned in the reformatory once again.

The next morning, the weather clears, the family is reunited, and Carmen, Alberto, and Jesús return to their subservient and loyal positions as wife, son, and foreman, respectively. As the family emerges from the kitchen into the sunlit courtyard, Buñuel can't resist inserting a little surrealist joke: Don Guadalupe looks up to the heavens and says, "It was all just like a bad dream." The camera dollies back out of the courtyard, through the gates of the hacienda, and into the surrounding countryside, revealing, from the outside, a self-contained, walled-in society that does in fact exist in a dream world.

Despite this pseudohappy ending, *Susana* begins and ends with the spectacle of a woman struggling violently against containment. More-

Figure 5.4. Susana (Rosita Quintana) is restrained by the political arm of the law and the social arm of patriarchy. *Susana,* production still.

over, in both the opening and the closing scene, it is the legal arm of patriarchy that holds the woman in check. This image of struggle works as a metaphor for a latent but central theme of *Susana:* the confrontation between human desire and social repression, a conflict that emerges repeatedly in the films of Buñuel.

Susana is perhaps one of the most unknowable cinematic femmes fatales because her secret is never revealed; it is ultimately locked up with her in her cell. Marsha Kinder writes that the sacrifice of a primary character in a parodic text "opens a space for radical change, not necessarily within the diegesis but within the signifying system" (1990, 74). Susana's promiscuity and her sexual assertiveness constitute a direct challenge to social and moral order. Though she is ultimately frustrated in all of her pursuits by sexual and social repression, it is at the expense of the narrative coherence, which then can be upheld only through Buñuel's surreal ending.

The happy ending, no matter how arbitrarily arrived at, is of course a convention of classical film melodrama. However, Franco suggests that paradoxical endings, which have no logical relation to the preceding sequence of narrative events, can work to "highlight the arbitrary nature of all narrative," including social narrative (1989, 135). Buñuel denies us the conventional "pleasure" of the classical melodrama by exposing the arbitrary nature not only of narratives but also of tradition and social mores. And Aranda perceptively argues that Buñuel's ending "has made us see that if we put ourselves on the side of the lubricious Susana and against these good Christians, it is because the spirit of justice is awakened in us, because finally he makes us discover where the positive values, and the truth, lie" (1976, 152).

Buñuel, Surrealism, and Parodic Critique

Despite recent critiques of the "author," we cannot categorically exclude a consideration of authorial intervention in the case of Buñuel. According to Robin Wood, a director's personal psychology often determines the level of thematic content to a certain extent (he gives the example of Hitchcock's recurring theme of "man's desire to dominate woman") (1988, 21). Wood does not deny that mainstream films are circumscribed by ideological constructions, by narrative patterns and generic conventions, and by other existing "forms, structures and conventions." However, he argues that the intervention of certain directors (he names Arthur Penn, John Ford, and Alfred Hitchcock, among others) can transform and appropriate these conventions. Although films cannot be reduced to an individual's "signature [or] touches," recognizable authorial marks emerge through thematic and stylistic repetitions across a body of work (1988, 12).

Similarly, Michel Foucault suggests that "the author's name is not simply a subject or predicate which can be replaced by a pronoun. . . . [I]t assumes a classificatory function . . . exceeding the limits of the texts" (1975, 606–607). For example, in the case of *Susana*, the term "Buñuel" signifies surrealism, and thus all the symbols, images, and aesthetic and political discourses surrounding the notion of surrealism inevitably intrude on discussions of Buñuel's films, whether they were produced in Spain, France, or Mexico.

Buñuel's history and his reputation were formed around a series of contradictions. First, although Spanish-born, he created his work outside of his native country, in France and Mexico; second, although he was well known as a surrealist filmmaker, most of his films were produced within the context of national commercial industries; and finally, as Marsha Kinder notes, though Buñuel made few films in Spain, he singularly represents Spanish film in most histories of that national cinema. In fact, Kinder has commented that Buñuel's experience best represents "the whole paradigm" of the émigré artist who leaves home "to satisfy curiosity, fame, or hunger; to find a more stimulating artistic environment or better economic opportunity; to escape oblivion, censorship, harassment, political persecution, or death" (1993, 287).

Although never a Mexican citizen, Buñuel is perhaps the best-known "Mexican" filmmaker outside of Mexico. He was almost forgotten when he arrived in Mexico in the late 1940s, but his 1950 film *Los olvidados* (*The Forgotten Ones*) brought Buñuel back into the international spotlight.[3] A film about the plight of street children living in the urban sprawl of Mexico City in the 1940s, *Los olvidados* was looked upon as more a Buñuelian film than a Mexican one, even by later film critics.[4] In fact, few critics have situated *Los olvidados* in the realm of Mexican cinema even though it was influenced by Buñuel's firsthand reaction to the effects of poverty and repression on the Mexican poor, and it was made within the Mexican film industry.

Altogether, Buñuel made more than twenty films in Mexico, including melodramas, comedies, and dramatic adaptations. Despite this relatively large body of work, most discussions of Buñuel do not consider his Mexican films in the context of Mexican cinema.[5] As noted above, Kinder regards Buñuel as the "paradigmatic case of exile" and suggests that the "hybridity" of his status clearly "demonstrates that nationality is an ideological construct" (1993, 286–287). While acknowledging that many of Buñuel's Mexican films are concerned with the legacy of colonialism, Kinder reads those films as products of "an exiled artist" and traces a "cultural continuity" across his Mexican and Spanish films, and a dialectical connection between these films and the ones he made in

France in the 1930s and then later in the 1960s and 1970s (1993, 292). She offers no analysis of the possible connection between the films Buñuel made in Mexico and Mexican cinema.

However, I think it is possible to consider Buñuel's *Susana* as an intervention in the cinematic representation of woman and sexual identity within Mexican cinema. According to Aranda, although in *Susana* "the conventions and vocabulary of the melodrama are respected," this respect does not "preclude a Surrealist vocabulary as well" (1976, 151–152). In Buñuel's Mexican films, the conventions of a national cinema are reworked to produce a critique of capitalism, patriarchy, the family, and the melodramatic mode itself through the use of surrealist and parodic strategies. Buñuel's exploitation of the femme fatale in films like *Susana* challenged traditional notions of female sexuality and the sacrosanct Mexican family. Within the economic and creative restraints inherent in working in a commercial film industry, Buñuel was able to produce some of his most powerful work. Using this opportunity to his advantage, he exposed the absurdities not only of social and sexual repression but also of cinematic melodrama. Aranda writes that Buñuel chose to work within the "popular language" of Mexican melodrama and rapidly "assimilated the national tradition of Mexican cinema" (1976, 144). In fact, Buñuel found the Mexican film melodrama to be a fertile domain in which to experiment with and subvert aesthetics and ideology.

He managed to introduce surrealistic images and tactics into many of his Mexican films. For instance, obscure references to animals and insects abound, dreamlike visions and experiences interrupt otherwise realistically rendered sequences, and normal human relations are suddenly inverted to reveal their constructed and arbitrary nature. In addition, melodramatic conventions are carried to extremes, gestures are heightened, and absurdities are exaggerated. All these tactics contribute to the subversion of melodramatic intent, which, according to D. N. Rodowick, seeks to find aesthetic solutions to ideological problems (1982, 41).

Buñuel's first Mexican film, *Gran casino* (1946), a musical starring the popular singer and actor Jorge Negrete and Argentina's Libertad Lamarque, was a failure at the box office. His second, a melodramatic comedy titled *El gran calavera* (1949), was a surprising box office success.

In 1949, Buñuel began working on *Los olvidados*, the film that rekindled his international prominence.

As in his earlier French surrealist films, Buñuel was always concerned with the political usefulness of his Mexican work. It was not enough that an audience reacted with pity to the myriad forms of human suffering; Buñuel wanted them to react with moral outrage.[6] Surrealism and parody were two strategies he employed to these ends. The purpose of surrealism, according to Buñuel, "was not to create a new literary, artistic, or even philosophical movement, but to explode the social order, to transform life itself" (1983, 107).

Founded by the writer André Breton and other French intellectuals, surrealism was an artistic and political movement that advocated the use of the dream state and other irrational states of mind to liberate human repression. On the one hand, believing that reality has multiple meanings, surrealists sought to create a language of artistic symbols. On the other hand, surrealism was also a political statement, a reaction against social repression characterized by conservative values of propriety and restraint. The expression of "forbidden" desires, such as eroticism and "mad passion" (*l'amour fou*), provided a means to state this opposition. The surrealists were revolutionaries of sorts, using humor, sex, and scandal as weapons to fight what they perceived to be the cultural, social, and political decadence of bourgeois society.

Although Buñuel has often been credited with introducing surrealism to Mexico in the 1940s, Breton had visited Mexico in 1938 and proclaimed it a "surrealist place *par excellence*" (Herrera, 1983, 226).[7] Hayden Herrera argues that the general Mexican audience was not "receptive" to surrealism because its members had their own forms of "magic and myths," and surrealism, for most Mexicans, represented a particularly European artistic movement. However, the work of Frida Kahlo and others attests to the fact that surrealism did have an impact on many Mexican artists, including some who had become disenchanted with the muralist movement, which privileged overt political themes over unconscious artistic impulses.[8]

Parody, unlike surrealism, is neither a genre nor a historical artistic movement. Moreover, it cannot be categorized as progressive or regressive in and of itself. According to the literary critic Joseph A. Dane, parody needs to be seen as a "form of criticism," a critical and purposeful subversion of a classical narrative system. In film, parody functions similarly as a purposeful critique of melodrama.

Rather than looking for radical forms of narrative constructions, Kinder suggests that directors like Wim Wenders and Rainer Werner Fassbinder employ parodic techniques of exaggeration, repetition, and excess to undermine traditional melodramatic representations. She writes that these parodic strategies "use the same signifiers to generate new meanings, creating an opposition between two signifying systems" (1990, 74).

In *Susana*, and in his other Mexican films, Buñuel appropriated conventions of cinematic melodrama and parodic strategies, both well integrated into the understanding of Mexican audiences. That Buñuel's films were readily absorbed into the classical Mexican cinema attests, on one level, to the pervasiveness of parody in Mexican discourse and, on another level, to the capacity of parody to bind to the conventions of the classical Mexican cinema.

In Mexico, parody takes on a particular cultural form, *la vacilada*, defined by Anita Brenner as melodrama at its most grotesque. She describes la vacilada as a strategy of caricature that "reverses values" and as an "untranslatable word . . . a trance [that] has served as simile for a strain, a tone, an attitude that runs through Mexican life" (1929, 180). Mexican parody surfaces in literature, art, and cultural practice as, on one hand, a state of continual doubt and, on the other hand, an acceptance of anything. The Mexican Day of the Dead (*el día de los muertos*), on which families exchange human skulls made of sugar and breads in the shape of skeletons, and Guadalupe Posada's distorted illustrations of Mexican *corridos* — etchings of skulls, fiends, and perverted creatures in the guise of human beings — are examples of la vacilada. Posada's parodic work illustrates that in order to confront the inevitability of death, Mexicans meet it head-on with exaggeration, celebration, and laughter, as if to say "I challenge you, I am not afraid."

It is often hard to uncover subversive strategies in melodramatic texts that, though shrouded in a layer of realism, generally manifest a surplus of stylistic and narrative excesses. However, when emotional expressions are revealed to be contrived, manipulative, and ridiculous, instead of natural and logical, and when customary melodramatic identification with characters is subverted, melodrama becomes parodic.[9]

In his Mexican films, Buñuel does not reject melodrama for social realism or avant-garde techniques. Instead, he uses the primary elements of melodrama—the opposition of good and evil, heightened emotional and physical expression—but intensifies them to the extent that they become hyperobvious. Thus, in *Susana,* while the characters align with the conventional roles in Mexican melodrama, their actions and motivations are exaggerated, subjective processes of identification are frustrated, and no one emerges as a hero. The spectator is denied emotional identification with all characters.

In addition, many narrative sequences are connected by unexpected incidents instead of logical and linear narrative links. This magnification of an existing melodramatic extravagance functions in *Susana* as a parodic critique of the melodramatic polarities and conventions of the classical Mexican cinema, and of the conventions of the bourgeois Mexican family. Polarities are exposed, conventions are overturned, the father is willing to give up his wife for an immoral young woman he has known for only a few days, and the virtuous and sacrificing mother turns into a vengeful and sadistic monster.

The character of Susana embodies the melodramatic elements being parodied in Buñuel's film. One might ask how she can be a central character in the narrative and at the same time embrace parodic strategies. Kinder offers an explanation for this kind of uncertainty by arguing that individual characters in parodic texts are "ambivalent signifiers," in that their meanings alternate between distinct signifying systems (in *Susana*'s case, between melodrama and surrealism), "revealing both the continuity and distance between them" (1990, 74). On the one hand, Susana is an excessively visual character who functions as the classic femme fatale in the Mexican family melodrama. She is the woman who inserts herself into the nuclear family, violently disrupting its moral and social order, only to be ultimately contained in order to preserve the familial structure and achieve narrative closure.

On the other hand, Susana is also a figure whose psychological motivations cannot be associated with any identifiable individual history. Seemingly the central protagonist of the narrative, she does not experience the psychological transformations associated with primary characters. Instead, she functions as a highly charged, overdetermined symbol of a sexuality that operates outside the bounds of social acceptability. While she is figuratively destroyed, as the femme fatale usually is, her removal leaves numerous narrative contradictions unresolved, despite the film's "happy" ending: The family remains as dysfunctional as it was before Susana arrived; the workers on the hacienda still live in unequal and repressive relation to their masters; and women still occupy the same subordinate position in relation to men.

In *Susana*, the family is exposed as a ravaged convention, tottering on weak legs of paternal control and moral uncertainty. Whereas the traditional Mexican family was presided over by an all-powerful father and submissive mother, in this film the father is presented as impotent and ineffectual, while the mother is perversely aggressive. Even the mother/child relationship is attacked. Alberto's relation with Doña Carmen resembles that of an angry young child to his mother, full of deceit on the one hand and guilt on the other. Buñuel exposes the empty values of tradition, duty, and habit, and Susana's aggressive sexuality eventually exposes the facade of this family. In doing so, she disrupts the entire social system of the hacienda.

Higgenbotham, writing that the hacienda serves as a microcosm of the Mexican social order, in which "labor serves management in a rigid capitalistic hierarchy" and women serve men in a similar patriarchal hierarchy, concludes that Susana's aggressive sexuality eventually challenges the fragile structure of the Mexican upper classes. However, in Buñuel's film, it is not that female sexuality in itself is threatening, as Higgenbotham seems to presume. Rather, it is that the family is so fragile that almost any external force will destroy its illusory stability, which functions within a false paradise of domesticity.

Thomas Schatz recognized that the Hollywood family melodrama emerged at a moment in the 1950s when the American middle-class family, "the clearest representation of America's patriarchal and bourgeois social order," was responding to economic and social changes brought about by the effects of World War II (1981, 226). The role of women, both inside and outside the family unit, became a central focus of American ideology and the Hollywood cinema. Mexican cinema reflected a similar crisis regarding the representation of sexual difference, the family, and woman in the 1940s.

The position of woman in narratives of change and the narrative coherence of the family in Mexican films in the 1940s were strained by the changing social status of the family in an era of booming industrialization, urbanization, and internal migration. The family thus came to represent an enigmatic and unstable structure in Mexican cinema. On the one hand, it was presented as necessary for maintenance of social order, while on the other hand, its instability also portrayed the disintegration of that order.

Franco, in her examination of Buñuel's *Los olvidados* (1950), notices that representations of fatherless families were occurring at a time when "the Mexican state [was] consolidating its paternal authority over its citizens" (1989, 154). While on the one hand, women had to continue to maintain the integrity of the family unit, on the other hand, if they were young, they had to be physically and emotionally strong enough to work outside the home, return at the end of the day to care for their family, and be a sexual partner for the husband or other male figure.

In an attempt to bolster a sense of coherence in a fragmented environment, postrevolutionary patriarchal discourses reemphasized the importance of familial relations, with the father as the head of the household and the state as head of the national family. The father's role was to assure his wife and children that the social, political, and moral promises of the Revolution were being fulfilled. However, as previously discussed, the failure of the state to provide real social and economic prosperity, combined with industrialization and the movement of large numbers of women out into the workforce, undermined this ideology. In films like *Susana* and *Doña Bárbara*, which removed the family from this ambivalent context and isolated it within the closed system of the hacienda, the weaknesses of the family, and thus of the national structure, which was dependent on the family's viability, were ultimately challenged, if not always destroyed.

The Desecrated Mother

In a number of Mexican films, la devoradora was pitted against the mother as a threat to the stability of the family. The figure of the mother was a central character in the classical Mexican film, usually portrayed as self-sacrificing, virtuous, and living only for the well-being of her family. Whereas the Hollywood maternal heroine of the 1930s and 1940s, played by actresses like Barbara Stanwyck, Bette Davis, and Loretta Young, was generally young, pretty, somewhat independent, and subject to the same weaknesses as other human beings, the Mexican mother, as personified by the actress Sara García, was most often older, past her prime in beauty as well as age, entrenched in her submissive role demanded by Mexican patriarchy, and, above all, absolutely virtuous. The narrative task of this mother was to hold her family together in the face of external threats, be they economic, physical, or sexual.

In both *Susana* and *Doña Bárbara* the power of the mother is intensified by the absence of a strong father figure. Laurencito, in *Doña Bárbara*, is an ineffectual and impotent drunkard who cannot support his daughter either economically or emotionally. In *Susana*, Don Guadalupe's guns and horses are more important to him than his family and his home. He leaves the business of the hacienda to Jesús, and of the home and family to his wife, Carmen.

What feminist criticism refers to as the "problem of the sexual mother" is overcome in *Susana* by desexing Doña Carmen. When her husband, overcome with lust for Susana, momentarily displaces his desire onto his wife, grabbing her and kissing her passionately, Doña Carmen pushes him away and looks around to make sure no one is watching. It is the only moment in the film in which a sexual relationship between husband and wife is represented. Their matrimonial bed is a place for dissention, and the dinner table is the site of larger familial relations.

Doña Bárbara and Susana, conversely, are always portrayed as "something else besides a mother." Susana, as a sexually desirable woman (or not-mother), is seemingly available for sex at any time of the day or night, at any conceivable location—including the barn, Alberto's bedroom, Don Guadalupe's study, and even the bottom of an empty well. Doña Bárbara, in the guise of the male, cannot be a mother by virtue of her assumed male identity and of her refusal to take on the social and emotional responsibilities of motherhood. However, female characters like Doña Bárbara and Susana were not offered other alternatives in the Mexican cinema. Thus, by the conclusion of both films, these figures had to be symbolically if not physically destroyed, because there was no other place to locate them.

Figure 5.5. Susana challenges the traditional role of women in Mexico. At the same time, she is femininity incarnate. *Susana*, production still.

If Doña Bárbara and Susana are ultimately denied a place in the narratives of these films, the figure of the "good mother" also suffers. She is absent in *Doña Bárbara* until the end, when her possibility reemerges in the figure of the young Marisela. In *Susana*, her alleged respectability is revealed to be just a mask. When Susana provokes Doña Carmen, suggesting that Don Guadalupe will choose her because she is young and beautiful, Doña Carmen, urged on by Perlita, begins to beat Susana viciously. Cutting to a low-angle shot, from the point of view of Susana, the camera looks up into the face of Doña Carmen, who, with a sadistic smile on her face, is obviously enjoying herself. The whipping will do nothing to restore family order. Indeed, when Don Guadalupe bursts in and grabs the whip from his wife, he assures Susana that she will not be the one forced to leave the hacienda. The whipping scene is the only time in the film where Doña Carmen is revealed to be capable of experiencing pleasure. The mother in *Susana,* though exposed as a sadistic and self-serving figure, is also a figure to be pitied.

La Devoradora: Femininity and Disguise

Both Susana and Doña Bárbara derive their limited and temporary power by means of disguise. While the notion of disguise has numerous connotations, in relation to sexual difference it involves an invocation of either masculinity or femininity. Joan Rivière, for example, alleges that a mask of femininity may be put on in order to "hide the possession of masculinity," (1966, 213). Doane, however, contests Rivière's analysis for suggesting that femininity does not exist and, if the masquerade is removed, nothing remains (1987, 34–37). Instead, Doane contends that a mask of femininity indicates the instability of the "feminine position" rather than its absence and that through disguise, women may actively select a site from which to stage their resistance by challenging the arbitrary assignment of sexual roles based on biological difference. According to Doane, then, masquerade, more than just a disguise, is an "acknowledgement that it is femininity itself which is constructed as a mask—as the decorative layer which conceals a non-identity" (1991, 25). Masquerade may thus be considered an intensification of gender and a "flaunting" of femininity.

Doane's hypothesis appears to destabilize the notion of masculine or feminine essence, while at the same time acknowledging the constructed nature of sexual difference. However, it still ignores the way in which a woman's appropriation of femininity as erotic spectacle may actually be an assertive act of power as well as a form of resistance. Through a strategy of masquerade, seduction becomes not merely a "weapon of the weak" but a vehicle whereby women may acquire access to patriarchal prerogatives.[10] As Doane reminds us, "the concepts of masculinity and femininity . . . have enormous socio-political implications and are linked to power" (1991, 38). This is why considerations of masquerade as a subversive gesture need to be examined in specific historical contexts.

I am arguing that masquerade can be seen as contesting, rather than merely denying, the positioning of the objectified and fetishized female body as the one and only form of femininity. This junction of femininity, disguise, and social discourse is one of the sites where Buñuel's parodic strategies surface in *Susana*. In this film, the masquerade of femininity constitutes a resistance from within, in the form of a purposefully invented facade that works to undermine the conventions of patriarchal social and narrative representation.

Susana is never presented as anything but a series of self-constructed expressions of femininity responding to individual male desire. According to the narrative, she has no history, no family, no psychic baggage, no individual identity that can be explained. As each of her masquerades is peeled off there is another disguise underneath. The creature revealed at the end of the film is not even human, resembling instead a trapped animal lashing out at those who would contain it.

For the men who desire her, Susana purposefully embodies all of the various elements of desirability assigned to woman. Whenever she enters the presence of Don Guadalupe, she pulls her blouse down, exposing her shoulders and the tops of her breasts. At the same time, she pretends to be innocent of the sexual passion she evokes in a man whose physical relations with his wife are nonexistent. When she is with Alberto, Susana is the virginal flirt who deliberately attempts to arouse her lover's desire, only to frustrate it. For Jesús, the virile and aggressive macho, Susana is the experienced woman who understands the animalistic nature of his sexuality.

Whereas Susana assumes a feminine disguise, Doña Bárbara, conversely, masquerades as a man. Claire Johnston, in her analysis of masquerade in Tourneur's film *Anne of the Indies*, suggests that the need to assume a masculine disguise by the female protagonist "indicates the absence of the male . . . [and] serves as a phallic substitute." Johnston writes that rather than simply covering up her femaleness, Anne "usurps" the power of the father. Similarly, I find that Doña Bárbara, like Anne, "is not just acting out a 'masculinity,' . . . she constitutes an utter and irrevocable refusal of 'femininity'" (1990, 66–67).

The primary feature of masquerade is costume, which has long been both a form of disguise for women and a visible sign that identifies gender and social status (uniforms, designer labels, etc.). In Doña Bárbara's case, clothes, like a mask, hide the female subject, and thus female desirability and female desire. Her split skirt, riding boots, whip, neck scarf, and holstered guns allow her to "be" a male in order to have access to powers traditionally denied women.

In *Doña Bárbara*, sexual ambiguity confuses the issue of sexual difference, exposing and challenging its constructed distinction. In order to "be" a man, Doña Bárbara must deny female sexuality and any sign of femininity. However, in this film, masquerade ultimately functions only as a temporary guise. Ideological and narrative conventions require that by the end of the film, men and women assume their "rightful" positions as a heterosexual, monogamous couple presiding over the Mexican family. Lacking the parodic critique of *Susana*, the ending of *Doña Bárbara* can only reaffirm Mexican patriarchy.

The representations of Susana and Doña Bárbara offered disturbing challenges to prevailing notions of femininity, female sexuality, and motherhood in the classical Mexican cinema, but, like the Hollywood femme fatale, they are ultimately restrained. However, while the devouring female figure in *Doña Bárbara* is finally subdued through narrative resolution, Susana can be suppressed only through a parodic deconstruction of both the melodramatic narrative and the classical representation of Mexican woman after almost destroying the familial, economic, and narrative systems of the family and the classical Mexican cinema.

I noted how the figure of la devoradora was part of Mexico's mythical and literary heritage. It is a telling sign that at numerous historical moments in Mexico, this figure has reemerged. According to Herrera-Sobek, the inclusion of such powerful and threatening female figures in dominant Mexican narrative and representational systems symbolizes the "struggle of the rebellious individual seeking to restructure the social canon and rupture those codes that stifled her freedom." Such a representation epitomizes a patriarchal ideology that is so conflicted, it can never be wholly successful in its attempt to exert absolute control (1990, 76). Women's desire for sexual, textual, and social freedoms can be contained but not annihilated. And as long as efforts to control women are mobilized, figures such as the femme fatale will surface to question and challenge the precariousness of patriarchal domination.

CONCLUSION

The films analyzed in this study are evidence of a collective attempt to renarrativize the position of woman in Mexican social discourse in the 1940s. This attempt was largely unsuccessful, however, because of the inability of the classical Mexican narrative structure to hold together in the face of the multiplicity of female subjectivity. Thus, I have suggested, for example, that the characters of Julieta, in *Distinto amanecer*, and Mercedes, in *Salón México*, may be seen not merely as portrayals of the Mexican dance-hall hostess, or of good women forced into compromising positions through economic hardship, but also as sites of the intersections of social and cultural ideology and cinematic practice. The various representations of woman in the six Mexican films discussed were generated by cinematic practices informed by the conventions of social relations and social discourses about sexual, ethnic, and class identities.

Although the films I looked at are not reflections of Mexican society, and although cinematic representations of women cannot be considered portraits of women in the audience, these films and their portrayals of femininity may be seen as products of, evidence of, and narrative responses to the material and psychic crisis permeating the Mexican nation, the same crises to which real Mexican women had to respond. The classical Mexican cinema thus gave narrative form and visual confirmation to real-life experience.

In my introduction, I broached the problem of the divided female subject. The previous chapters have demonstrated that in Mexican cultural representations, this divided subject is specifically Mexican. In *The Two Fridas* (1939), Frida Kahlo presented a double image of her self: the first, a white, Europeanized mestiza Frida, wears a Victorian dress; the second is clothed in a Tehuana Indian skirt and blouse.

The representations of woman in the classical Mexican cinema, like Kahlo's self-portraits, reveal the paradoxical dilemma of confirming one's own subjectivity (for both men and women). On the one hand is the ideological insistence that society and the individual recognize subjectivity as unitary, while on the other hand is the realization that individual consciousness is subject to multiple determining pressures of historical, social, and psychic forces.

I have used the classical Mexican cinema to explore how cinematic representations, within the context of a specific national cinema, work to negotiate these complex relations between society and the gendered individual. For feminist film critics, moments of social crisis offer a fertile ground for the investigation of the "woman question" in national cinemas. In her examination of Soviet silent films of the 1920s, for example, Judith Mayne finds that period in Soviet history to be a critical moment in the reformulation of discourses surrounding sex and gender. Although she does situate early Soviet cinema in the historical context of the Soviet socialist political project and does not ignore the relation between art and politics, Mayne's study differs significantly from most histories of Soviet cinema in that her focus is on the way in which the films explore what she terms "woman's position within socialist culture" (1989, 1). Mayne argues that such an approach "offers a critical vantage point from which to comprehend the narrative strategies central to the development of Soviet cinema; and, similarly, that these narrative strategies are central to an understanding of the representation of women in relation to cultural and political change" (1989, 15). The significance of Mayne's approach for my investigation of Mexican cinema lies at this junction of politics, gender, and aesthetics. The portrayal of woman in Mexican cinema in the 1940s worked both to reveal and to problematize the contradictory discourses surrounding the position of women in Mexican postrevolutionary family and social life.

In closing, I would like to suggest where I think this work fits in the general field of film studies. First, it will enlarge the slim body of literature about a national cinema with a vibrant history. Critics have paid little attention to the Mexican cinema, often lumping it together with the rest of Latin American film. Until recently, only so-called revolutionary cinemas—Cuban cinema and Brazilian Cinema Novo, for example—have merited much consideration. However, with the recent attention toward popular culture and the consideration of melodrama as a worthwhile object of critical study, the histories of other national cinemas are being looked at with new regard: not merely in relation to the dominance of the classical Hollywood system, but as "interventions" in the canonical narrative of world cinema.

Second, the study will contribute to the ongoing exploration of the diverse and distinctive ways in which national cinemas represent woman and femininity, as well as the various ways in which woman and femininity emerge in national cinemas to challenge the conflicted discourses of patriarchy in its incalculable manifestations. Looking at nationality and femininity in British postwar films, Antonia Lant asks "how femininity might be constructed differently across different national cinemas, and indeed, how national identity might be imaged through different versions of femininity" (1991, 15). Feminist analyses of national cinemas can reveal not only other forms of femininity, of patriarchal expression, and of psychic forms and archetypes, but also other patterns of narrative resistance. Such studies may also enlarge the way in which we look at and analyze the representation of sexual difference and woman in our own cinemas, contributing not only to a broadening of feminist scholarship but also to a deepening of it.

Third, this inquiry will stimulate a reevaluation of the way film scholars look at national cinema practices. Rather than simply arguing that Western critics cannot write about the Third World or other cultures because of histories of conquest and imperialism, and/or racial differences, I think it is more productive to talk about ways in which we may offer interpretations that are acknowledged as being partial and limited but nonetheless are useful and elegant. I submit this study of the representation of woman in Mexican film in the 1940s as such an interpretation.

And, finally, I hope the foregoing analyses have demonstrated the complexity of locating answers to the question of the representation of gendered identity. Those who claim that woman is *always* a sign of instability ignore the fundamental fluidity of human consciousness and its power to shape reality. As Raymond Williams has argued, the making of signs, and of signification or meaning, is a "practical material activity" that "is involved from the beginning in all other human social and material activity." While this is not meant to suggest that meaning is produced by individuals solely from the content of personal experience, I submit, following Williams, that the social nature of signification needs to be seen as a dialectical process that is "necessarily connected with the social and material as well as the formal dynamics of the system as a whole" (1977, 38–43). Williams's reminder applies not only to cinema but also to our analyses of cinema.

NOTES

Introduction

1. See Fredric Jameson's *Political Unconscious* (1991, ch. 1).

2. A number of other writers have contributed shorter essays and articles, including Ana M. López (1985 and 1991), Susan Dever (1992), and Carmen Huaco-Nuzum (1992).

3. In an early study of women in Hollywood film, Molly Haskell writes, "In the dark melodramas of the forties, woman came down from her pedestal [of the thirties] and she didn't stop when she reached the ground" (1974, 189). See also E. Ann Kaplan's collection, *Women in Film Noir* (1980), for various responses to the function of woman in Hollywood film noir narratives during the war years. For studies of the representation of women in British melodrama see especially Antonia Lant's *Blackout* (1991).

4. See Patrice Petro's *Joyless Streets* (1989).

Chapter 1. The Timeless Paradox: Mother and Whore

1. I would like to thank Charles Ramirez Berg for pointing out to me the notion of "ready-made" narratives in relation to Mexican gendered relations.

2. This understanding of archetype is very similar to Mikhail Bakhtin's theory of genre. Bakhtin writes that genres, like all cultural and literary traditions, are preserved and continue to live, not in the subjective memory of the individual or in some collective "psyche," but in the objective forms of culture itself (quoted in Todorov, 1984, 85).

3. See León-Portilla's *Broken Spears* (1992), an edited summary of written accounts of the Spanish conquest by various Aztec writers. León-Portilla reminds us that these accounts were not only historical, but also mythological, in that the Aztecs believed the arrival of the Spanish had been foretold as the coming of the Aztec god Quetzalcoatl.

See also Tzvetan Todorov's *Conquest of America* (1984) for an analysis of documents produced at the time of the Spanish conquest by both the Spanish and the indigenous peoples. Todorov's interest is in the documents not as actions of individual authors but as "sources of information about a reality of which they do not constitute a part." The productions and revelations of the documents are not as important to Todorov as is the history of their reception. He writes that "the reception of the statements is more revealing for the history of ideologies than their production; and when an author is mistaken, or lying, his text is no less significant than when he is speaking the truth. . . .

From this point of view, the notion of 'false' is irrelevant here" (1984, 53–54). In the same way, I am not so much concerned with the "truth" of the relations between La Malinche and Cortés as I am with the way these relations have been represented.

4. Although La Malinche is condemned for her betrayal, her relationship with Cortés is also remembered as the union that produced the first Mexican mestizo, Martín Cortés.

5. See, for example, Adelaide Del Castillo and Magdalena Mora's *Mexican Women in the United States* (1980) and Gloria Anzaldúa's *Borderlands/La Frontera* (1987).

6. See Jacques Lafaye's "Guadalupe, a Mexican National Emblem" (1976) for a chronicle of the Virgin's rise to recognition in the Mexican Catholic Church.

7. See Ilene O'Malley's *Myth of the Revolution* (1986), and Elizabeth Salas' *Soldaderas in the Mexican Military* (1990).

8. According to Vasconcelos, "racial fusion," as he termed the mixture of cultures, would be "naturally" governed by the highest sense of "aesthetic taste": "The very ugly will not procreate, they will have no desire to procreate. . . . Poverty, defective education, the scarcity of beautiful types, the misery that makes people ugly, all those calamities will disappear from the future social stage" (1979, 28).

9. Whereas in the United States, women's entry into the labor force during the 1940s is explained by the impact of World War II, this was not the case in Mexico, which did not officially enter the war, although a number of Mexican men served under U.S. command.

Chapter 2. Mexican Cinema and the Woman Question

1. The strongest sector of the domestic industry, in fact, was the distributors. Mexican entrepreneurs had discovered that it was more profitable and less risky to invest in distribution than in production. However, as I will discuss later, by the 1920s, Hollywood controlled this sector of the industry.

2. In comparison, Chile produced 54 silent films between 1902 and 1932; in Brazil, between 1898 and 1930, 1,685 films were produced (Armes, 1987, 166–167).

3. Through a process of vertical integration, a few companies secured control of all three aspects of the motion picture industry in the United States: production, distribution, and exhibition. With a guaranteed and sizable domestic market in which to recoup production costs, these major companies turned to foreign distribution to expand their profits. In 1927, Sidney R. Kent, general manager of the Paramount-Famous-Lasky Corporation, noted that "out of every dollar received, seventy-five cents comes out of America and only twenty-five cents comes out of all the foreign countries combined." However, "the profit in these pictures is in that last twenty-five percent" (Kent, 1927, 228).

4. In 1939, Hollywood was dependent on export markets for 35 to 40 percent of its film rentals (*Motion Picture Herald*, March 18, 1939, 17).

5. See Hershfield's "Paradise Regained" (1996).

6. Marie Seton, one of Eisenstein's biographers, also refers to the influence of Mexican artists on *Que viva México!*, writing that one of Eisenstein's compositions "was a dynamic interpretation of David Alfaro Siqueiros' unfinished and mutilated fresco, *Burial of a Worker*" (1952, 198). Moreover, according to Eisenstein's own notes, a never-finished section of the film was to have been based on Orozco's fresco *Las soldaderas*.

7. The Golden Age of Mexican cinema was also affected by the immigration of half a million refugees from the Spanish Civil War. These artists, writers, and filmmakers made their mark in Mexican art, literature, and cinema between 1939 and 1959. Alejandro Galindo argues that the contribution of these Spanish refugees was "negative" (1985, 27-28). Galindo also suggests that the 1933 film directed by Arcady Boytler, *La mujer del puerto*, is not a Mexican film because Boytler was not a Mexican (he was a Russian émigré) and the film was based on stories by Maupassant and Tolstoy. However, other critics, most notably Monsiváis, have commended Boytler's film as *"el primer film mexicano singular, absolutamente personal"* (quoted in García Riera, 1969, I, 54). This argument poses complex questions about the influence of individual authorship, an issue to which I turn in chapter 5 in my discussion of Luis Buñuel, a Spanish "refugee."

8. These new theatrical practices launched a number of future cinema stars, such as Mario Moreno (more popularly known as Cantinflas), and influenced acting styles in Mexican silent and sound films (Lamb, 1975, 9).

9. In his discussion of the classical Hollywood cinema, for example, Thomas Schatz writes that a genre film evidences "the cooperation between artists and audience in celebrating their collective values and ideals," considered within the sociocultural context of its production (1981, 15).

10. Ravi Vasudevan, for example, finds that Hindi cinematic melodrama in the 1950s reaffirms woman as primarily a mother figure, serving as a "regressive fantasy" for the male hero (1989, 34). Antonia Lant focuses on the particular relations represented in British cinema during World War II between national identity and British femininity, in order to situate the changing representations of femininity in the British context. She finds that at times of national crisis, such as war, the need to strengthen the notion of a national identity seems urgent. However, as Lant reminds us, "the specificity of socio-cultural and national milieus militates against the assignation of fixed meanings to aesthetic codes" (1991, 157).

Chapter 3. Cinema, Woman, and National Identity

1. See, for example, Antonia Lant's *Blackout* (1991).

2. Translated literally, *la madre patria* means "motherland." However, as Amy K. Kaminsky points out, though the phrase's grammatical gender is designated as female (through the use of *madre* and the feminine *la*), "*patria* is rooted in the notion of the father" (1993, 5). Translated literally, *patria* means "fatherland." As Kaminsky argues,

this example of grammatical ambiguity epitomizes one of the problems of language in cross-cultural analysis. For a thorough discussion of the specificity of this problem for Latin Americanist feminists, see her introduction to *Reading the Body Politic* (1993).

3. According to the historian Alan Knight, the Spanish initially attempted to maintain cultural and biological distinctions between Indians and Spanish immigrants but were unsuccessful. During Spanish rule, the term "Indian" came to refer to a "fiscal" or class category rather than an ethnic one. By the time of Porfirio Díaz's rise to power in 1876, the majority of Mexicans were mestizo (of mixed blood), and social and ethnic classifications were subsequently defined through a confluence of categories including "language, dress, religion, social organization, culture, and consciousness" (1990, 72–73). Though many groups still viewed themselves as Indian, carried on local and regional traditions, and spoke indigenous languages, their needs were ignored in order to further the needs of "the nation."

4. According to Benedict Anderson, because the invented "naturalness" of "nationalism" implies a disinterest on the part of the state, the state can therefore request individual sacrifice for the good of all citizens (1983, 131–132). In fact, he argues that the character of nationalism is based on notions of a "self-sacrificing" love for *la patria* (129).

5. See Julia Tuñón's *En su propio espejo* (1988).

6. Ann Pescatello points out that in most Latin American countries, class differences and differences between rural and urban structures need to be taken into account when analyzing the situation of women. She argues that the lower-class urban woman usually had "much more autonomy and prerogatives since her husband spent little time in the home," thus guaranteeing "more social fluidity." However, although women in the rural sector of the economy may have occupied a more primary role in the "economic and social milieu," their access to social mobility was more limited (something they shared with poor rural males) because of factors such as "illiteracy, poor health, lack of communication" (1976, 198). Pescatello, however, fails to consider the additional factor of race and the way in which it compounded the oppression of lower-class, rural women.

7. In an essay on the Mexican director María Elena Velasco, Carmen Huaco-Nuzum suggests that the light-skinned Del Rio "masquerades as an indigenous woman" in Fernández's films about Mexico's indigenous populations and represents the "neo-indigenism of Mexican national culture." She argues that such a masquerade created a "representational gap that must have impeded a large section of the indigenous and *mestiza* population from directly identifying with her character" (1992, 129). However, I would suggest that spectators' identifications and understandings are not grounded solely on their perception of visual images. There are other processes involved in the production of meaning in the relation among text, spectator, and context.

8. Like many Hollywood stars, Félix's off-screen life came to be identified with her on-screen persona. Richard Dyer, for example, finds a "high degree of interpene-

tration" between Lana Turner's public and private lives, a coupling other critics have noted in regard to Bette Davis, Joan Crawford, and Marlene Dietrich (1986, 31).

9. Susan Dever discusses how, even today, Félix functions as a "cultural mediator whose discourse will be controlled by the kind of roles she is permitted to play." She describes how the figure of Félix, dressed in "Amazon garb," has recently been "deployed . . . to mediate" the Indian question in modern-day Mexico (1992, 62–63).

10. *María Candelaria* was the first Mexican film to be recognized at an international film festival (Cannes, in 1946).

11. Octavio Paz attempted to absolve the Spanish by suggesting that they were "not quite as bad" as the English. Though he admits that Spain did commit "many horrors . . . at least it did not commit the gravest of all: that of denying a place, even at the foot of the social scale, to the people who composed it" (1985, 103). Spain's greatest contribution to Mexico, according to Paz, was the creation of a "universal order," which he apparently assumed did not exist before the conquest.

12. The term "caciquismo" refers to peasant agricultural organizations that began during Spanish rule. Under this system, land is provided by the state for the peasants to farm, but the cacique, a kind of Mexican godfather, is appointed to oversee agricultural production. Cockcroft argues that the system "blurs class consciousness" through an ideology of a cooperative system where the boss and the workers are interdependent (1983, 203). In reality, the "cooperatives" operated as enclosed feudal systems under the control of the cacique. Under President Alemán, the land reforms of the Cárdenas administration were reversed. Alemán reinstated economic protection for private landowners and enlarged the legal size of landholdings, and he authorized the breakup of cooperative peasant land operations. Although agricultural exports increased, landholdings and profits were concentrated in large farms at the expense, again, of landless rural peasants.

13. See Jesús Martín-Barbero's *Communication, Culture, and Hegemony*, especially part 3, "Modernization and Mass Mediation in Latin America," for a discussion of what he terms "the discontinuity between the state and the nation."

14. After carefully analyzing the representations of men and women in Eisenstein's *Potemkin*, for instance, Mayne writes in *Kino and the Woman Question* (1989) that the film demonstrates "how in the practice of montage, there is a persistent sexual dynamic at work" (43). Mayne's larger argument is that although Soviet films were intended to "produce" socialism, the narratives often reproduced structures of sexual opposition, regardless of the extent to which directors employed the use of dialectical montage.

15. Janet Staiger pointed out to me how this structure is much like the convention of the Hollywood western genre, only reversed. In the western, men are aligned with nature and women with civilization.

16. Though the Revolution had been profoundly anticlerical, and initial postrevolutionary presidents retained this view, Miguel Alemán took office in 1946 claiming

that he was a "believer," thereby reinstating the Church's position in Mexican social relations.

17. According to Ramirez Berg, this portrayal "is due to the contradictory nature of the Church's presence in Mexican life," where it is both venerated and resented (1992a, 27).

18. The distinctive Fernández/Figueroa style is described in detail by Ramirez Berg in his study of the development of the classical Mexican cinematographic style. See "Figueroa's Skies and Oblique Perspective: Notes on the Development of the Classical Mexican Style," *Spectator* 13 (spring 1992): 21–41. In summary, these elements included composition in depth, a complex mise-en-scène with multiple planes of action, and the use of low-angle shots. Ramirez Berg focuses on Fernández and Figueroa's use of curvilinear or oblique perspective as opposed to Hollywood's reliance on linear perspective, derived from traditions in Western art. What is most important about Ramirez Berg's analysis is its emphasis on the alignment between ideology and aesthetic practice. Thus, according to Ramirez Berg, the Fernández/Figueroa "style" is important not only for its contribution to the creation of a specifically Mexican cinema but also for its challenge of "Western artistic traditions and the dominant ideology they conveyed" (1992b, 39).

Chapter 4. The Cinema of the *Cabaretera*

1. The Mexican cabaretera films share certain stylistic, thematic, and representational elements with film noir, though many of them were produced a number of years before most of the Hollywood films. *Distinto amanecer,* released in 1943, for example, was replete with corruption, shadowy figures, dark staircases, oblique angles, and confused protagonists, and even foreshadowed the conflicted and fatalistic narrative resolutions of film noir of the late 1940s and early 1950s. These Mexican films also prefigured film noir's contested representations of woman in a shifting social environment. In addition, García Riera suggests that *Distinto amanecer* and other films with a similar visual style were inspired, in part, by the French poetic realism of Carne and Prevert (1986, 142). It also is generally acknowledged that film noir itself was influenced by German expressionism brought by German directors, cinematographers, and art directors during the 1930s.

2. My use of the notion of desire here refers to that larger scope of human yearning which encompasses more than merely the hunger for sex. Desire also functions in the struggle for material and emotional needs, and it is on this level that I explore the woman question in *Salón México*.

3. As has been noticed by every critic who has reviewed *Distinto amanecer,* the film playing in the cinema is Bracho's earlier film, *Ay, qué tiempos, señor don Simón!* (1941), an upbeat musical that was the biggest Mexican box office hit of the year.

4. Although it is never explicitly stated that Julieta is a prostitute and engages in sexual relations with men for money, her obvious distaste for her work and for the men for whom she must provide pleasure indicates that in the sphere of economics, women's bodies are bought and sold in ways that do not preclude sexual intercourse.

5. There is a similar scene in *Mildred Pierce*. However, *Distinto amanecer* was released three years before the Hollywood film. This coincidence is perhaps indicative of the pervasiveness of the conflicted territory between class and gender across cultural and temporal boundaries.

6. Salón México was an area in Mexico City famous for its nightclubs. The area inspired Aaron Copeland to write a musical suite of the same name, and in fact this is revealed in the film during a moment that seems to foreground the influence of Mexican culture on the United States, instead of vice versa.

7. See, for example, Carmen Huaco-Nuzum's *"Ni de aquí, ni de allá"* (1992), Norma Alarcón's "Theoretical Subject(s) of *This Bridge Called My Back* and Anglo-American Feminism" (1990), and Rosa Linda Fregosa and Angie C. Chabram's "Introduction: Chicana/o Cultural Representations" (1990). See also Tania Modleski's "Cinema and the Dark Continent" (1991) and Jane Gaines's *"Scar of Shame"* (1989) for more general Anglo-feminist criticism of the absence of race in feminist discussions.

Chapter 5. *La Devoradora*: The Mexican Femme Fatale

1. It may be coincidental, but it is interesting to note that *bárbaro* in Spanish means barbarous or savage.

2. In her *Foundational Fictions* (1991), Doris Sommer devotes a chapter to the analysis of Gallegos' novel as an erotic narrative about the formation of Venezuelan national identity.

3. His last major film, *Las hurdes*, released in the United States as *Land without Bread*, had been made in 1933. After that, Buñuel had made a few commercial comedies in Spain and had been a dubbing director for Warner Brothers in Hollywood.

4. For example, Robert P. Kolker has suggested that because Mexican audiences would not accept surrealism, Buñuel used neorealism to achieve commercial viability. Despite this premise, Buñuel rejected neorealism, saying that it was "incomplete, official and above all reasonable," all of which were contrary to the demands of surrealism (1983, 95). Indeed, Buñuel noted, "All that completes and enlarges tangible reality, is completely absent from its works" (quoted in Matthews, 1971, 140). While *Los olvidados* may evidence neorealist tendencies, they are more clearly traceable to the influences of Buñuel's earlier surrealistic and parodic film, *Las hurdes* (1932).

5. Although John King argues that Buñuel's influence is almost nonexistent in Mexican films after 1960, Ramirez Berg points to the work of Luis Alcoriza, a collaborator of Buñuel's for more than thirteen years. Of Alcoriza, Ramirez Berg writes that

his "debt to Buñuel is inconsiderable. . . . His films are a mixture of existential, surrealist, and absurdist elements" (1992a, 183).

6. Although he attacked Catholicism and all religions in his films, Buñuel remained a strong moralist all his life, writing that "bourgeois morality is for me immorality, against which one must fight. Morality [is] founded on our very unjust social institutions, like religion, patriotism, the family, culture; in brief, what are called the 'pillars' of society" (Matthews, 1971, 142).

7. While staying with Frida Kahlo and her husband, Diego Rivera, during his visit to Mexico, Breton became an ardent admirer of Kahlo's work and arranged a show for her in Paris the following year. In 1940, Breton organized the International Exhibition of Surrealism in Mexico City and included the work of Kahlo and other Mexican artists. According to Breton, Kahlo was the Mexican artist who exhibited the strongest surrealistic impulse, though she wrote, "I never knew I was a Surrealist" until Breton told her she was (quoted in Herrera, 1983, 254).

8. My thanks to Mary Desjardins for reminding me that surrealists, like some Mexican postrevolutionary artists, exhibited a fascination with primitive art. Kahlo and Rivera, for instance, incorporated pre-Columbian themes and motifs into their work.

9. My discussion of the parodic deconstruction of melodrama should not be confused with what Thomas Schatz refers to as the parodic or self-reflexive stage of a film genre, in which a genre's basic aesthetic values are called into question. Schatz writes that "throughout a genre's evolution from transparent social reaffirmation to opaque self-reflexivity, there is a gradual shift in narrative emphasis from social value to formal aesthetic value" (1981, 40–41).

10. See James C. Scott's *Weapons of the Weak* (1985). Scott argues that received history, both Marxist and traditional, has tended to mark only those moments of resistance in which a direct threat to the state or world order has been posed. Scott is more interested in "everyday resistance," what he sees as the "constant struggle" between the dominated and the dominant. He interprets such tactics as foot-dragging, false compliance, slander, and sabotage as "weapons of the weak," forms of passive struggle that are neither coordinated nor directed, and frequently are concerned with the needs of the individual. This type of resistance seems particularly relevant to Third World societies that have not developed through the trajectory of the capitalist narrative predicted by Marx but instead have been defined by conquest, colonization, peasant social structures, and patriarchy.

BIBLIOGRAPHY

Alarcón, Norma. 1990. "The Theoretical Subject(s) of *This Bridge Called My Back* and Anglo-American Feminism." In *Making Face, Making Soul*, ed. Gloria Anzaldúa. San Francisco: Aunt Lute Foundation Books.

Anderson, Benedict. 1983. *Imagined Communities.* London: Verso.

Anzaldúa, Gloria. 1987. *Borderlands/La Frontera: The New Mestiza.* San Francisco: Spinsters/Aunt Lute.

Aranda, Francisco. 1976. *Luis Buñuel: A Critical Biography.* Trans. and ed. David Robinson. New York: Da Capo Press.

Armes, Roy. 1987. *Third World Filmmaking and the West.* Berkeley: University of California Press.

Ayala Blanco, Jorge. 1968. *La aventura del cine mexicano.* Mexico City: Ediciones Era.

Bartra, Roger. 1992. *The Cage of Melancholy: Identity and Metamorphosis in the Mexican Character.* Trans. Christopher J. Hall. New Brunswick, N.J.: Rutgers University Press.

Bordwell, David. 1985. *Narration in the Fiction Film.* Madison: University of Wisconsin Press.

Bradway, E. 1984. *Prophecy and Myth in Mexican History.* Cambridge: Centre of Latin American Studies, University of Cambridge.

Brenner, Anita. 1929. *Idols behind Altars.* Boston: Beacon Press.

Brooks, Peter. 1976. *The Melodramatic Imagination: Balzac, Henry James, Melodrama and the Mode of Excess.* New Haven, Conn.: Yale University Press.

Buñuel, Luis. 1983. *My Last Sigh.* Trans. Abigail Israel. New York: Alfred A. Knopf.

Chant, Sylvia. 1991. *Women and Survival in Mexican Cities: Perspectives on Gender, Labour Markets and Low-Income Households.* Manchester, U.K.: Manchester University Press.

Cline, Howard F. 1963. *Mexico: Revolution to Evolution: 1940–60.* New York: Oxford University Press.

Cockcroft, James D. 1983. *Mexico: Class Formation, Capital Accumulation, and the State.* New York: Monthly Review Press.

Cook, Pam. 1989. "Melodrama and the Women's Picture." In *Imitations of Life: A Reader on Film and Television Melodrama*, ed. Marcia Landy. Detroit: Wayne State University Press.

Cypess, Sandra Messinger. 1991. *La Malinche in Mexican Literature: From History to Myth.* Austin: University of Texas Press.

Dane, Joseph A. 1990. "An Overview of Directions in Contemporary Criticism of Literary Parody." *Quarterly Review of Film and Video* 12: 135–139.

De Lauretis, Teresa. 1984. *Alice Doesn't: Feminism, Semiotics, Cinema*. Bloomington: Indiana University Press.

———. 1986. "Feminist Studies, Critical Studies: Issues, Terms, and Contexts." In *Feminist Studies/Critical Studies*, ed. Teresa De Lauretis. Bloomington: Indiana University Press.

Del Castillo, Adelaida, and Magdalena Mora. 1980. *Mexican Women in the United States: Struggles Past and Present*. Los Angeles: Chicano Studies Research Publications.

Dever, Susan. 1992. "Re-Birth of a Nation: On Mexican Movies, Museums, and Maria Felix." *Spectator* 13 (fall): 52–69.

Doane, Mary Ann. 1987. *The Desire to Desire*. Bloomington: Indiana University Press.

———. 1991. *Femmes Fatales: Feminism, Film Theory, Psychoanalysis*. New York: Routledge.

Dyer, Richard. 1986. *Heavenly Bodies: Film Stars and Society*. New York: St. Martin's Press.

Eisenstein, Sergei. 1971. *Que viva México!* 2nd ed. Mexico City: Ediciones Eras.

Elsaesser, Thomas. 1986. "Tales of Sound and Fury: Observations on the Family Melodrama." In *Film Genre Reader*, ed. Barry Keith Grant. Austin: University of Texas Press.

Fisher, Lillian Estelle. 1942. "The Influence of the Present Mexican Revolution upon the Status of Mexican Women." *Hispanic American Historical Review* 22, no. 1 (Feb.): 211–228.

Foucault, Michel. 1975. "What Is an Author?" Trans. James Venat. *Partisan Review* 42, no. 4: 603–614.

Franco, Jean. 1989. *Plotting Women: Gender and Representation in Mexico*. New York: Columbia University Press.

Fregosa, Rosa Linda, and Angie C. Chabram. "Introduction: Chicana/o Cultural Representations: Reframing Alternative Critical Discourse." *Cultural Studies* 4, no. 3 (October 1990): 203–212.

Gaines, Jane. 1989. "*The Scar of Shame*: Skin Color and Caste in Black Silent Melodrama." In *Imitations of Life*, ed. Marcia Landy. Detroit: Wayne State University Press.

Galindo, Alejandro. 1985. *El cine mexicano: Un personal punto de vista*. Mexico: EDAMEX.

García Riera, Emilio. 1963. *El cine mexicano*. Mexico City: Ediciones Era.

———. 1969. *Historia documental del cine mexicano*. I, 1926–1940; II, 1941–1944; III, 1945–1948; IV, 1949–1951; V, 1952–1954. Mexico City: Ediciones Era.

———. 1974. *El cine y su público*. Mexico: FCF.

———. 1986. *Historia del cine mexicano, 1926–1966*. 9 vols. Mexico City: Ediciones SEP.

Gledhill, Christine. 1987. "The Melodramatic Field: An Investigation." In *Home Is Where the Heart Is: Studies in Melodrama and the Woman's Film*, ed. Christine Gledhill. London: BFI.

———. 1991. "Signs of Melodrama." In *Stardom: Industry of Desire*, ed. Christine Gledhill. London: Routledge.

González Salazar, Gloria. 1980. "Participation of Women in the Mexican Labor Force." In *Sex and Class in Latin America: Women's Perspectives on Politics, Economics and the Family in the Third World,* ed. June Nash and Helen Icken Safa. South Hadley, Mass.: J. F. Bergin.

Hartmann, Susan M. 1982. *The Homefront and Beyond: American Women in the 1940s.* Boston: Twayne.

Haskell, Molly. 1974. *From Reverence to Rape: The Treatment of Women in the Movies.* Harmondsworth, U.K.: Penguin.

Hellman, Judith Adler. 1978. *Mexico in Crisis.* New York: Holmes and Meier.

Helpren, Morris. 1932. "*Que viva México!:* Eisenstein in Mexico." *Experimental Cinema* 4.

Herrera, Hayden. 1983. *Frida: A Biography of Frida Kahlo.* New York: Harper & Row.

Herrera-Sobek, Maria. 1990. *The Mexican Corrido: A Feminist Analysis.* Bloomington: Indiana University Press.

Hershfield, Joanne. 1992. "The Construction of 'Woman' in *Distinto amanecer.*" *Spectator* 13, no. 1 (fall): 42–51.

———. 1996. "Paradise Regained: Eisenstein's *Que Viva Mexico!* as Ethnography." In *Documenting the Documentary,* ed. Barry K. Grant and Jeannette Sloniowksi. Detroit: Wayne State University Press.

Higgenbotham, Virginia. 1979. *Luis Buñuel.* Boston: Twayne.

Huaco-Nuzum, Carmen. 1992. "*Ni de aquí, ni de allá:* Indigenous Female Representation in the Films of María Elena Velasco." In *Chicanos and Film: Representation and Resistance,* ed. Chon Noriega. Minneapolis: University of Minnesota Press.

Jameson, Fredric. 1991. *The Political Unconscious: Narrative as a Socially Symbolic Act.* Ithaca, N.Y.: Cornell University Press.

Johnston, Claire. 1990. "Femininity and the Masquerade: *Anne of the Indies.*" In *Psychoanalysis and Cinema,* ed. E. Ann Kaplan. New York: Routledge.

Kaminsky, Amy K. 1993. *Reading the Body Politic: Feminist Criticism and Latin American Woman Writers.* Minneapolis: University of Minnesota Press.

Kaplan, E. Ann. 1980. "The Place of Women in Fritz Lang's *The Blue Gardenia.*" In *Women in Film Noir,* ed. E. Ann Kaplan. Rev. ed. London: BFI.

———. 1983. *Women and Film: Both Sides of the Camera.* New York: Methuen.

———. 1990. "Motherhood and Representation: From Postwar Freudian Figurations to Postmodernism." In *Psychoanalysis and Cinema,* ed. E. Ann Kaplan. New York: Routledge.

Kent, Sidney R. "Distributing the Product." In *The Story of Films,* ed. Joseph P. Kennedy. Chicago: A. W. Shaw Company, 1927.

Kinder, Marsha. 1990. "Ideological Parody in the New German Cinema: Reading *The State of Things, The Desire of Veronika Voss,* and *Germany Pale Mother* as Postmodernist Rewritings of *The Searchers, Sunset Boulevard,* and *Blonde Venus.*" *Quarterly Review of Film and Video* 12: 73–103.

———. 1993. *Blood Cinema: The Reconstruction of National Identity in Spain.* Berkeley: University of California Press.

King, John. 1990. *Magical Reels: A History of Cinema in Latin America.* London: Verso.

King, John, Ana M. López, and Manuel Alvarado, eds. 1993. *Mediating Two Worlds: Cinematic Encounters in the Americas.* London: BFI.

Knight, Alan. 1990. "Racism, Revolution, and Indigenismo: Mexico, 1920-1940." In *The Idea of Race in Latin America, 1870–1940,* ed. Richard Graham. Austin: University of Texas Press.

Kolker, Robert P. 1983. *The Altering Eye: Contemporary International Cinema.* New York: Oxford University Press.

Kozloff, Sarah. 1989. *Invisible Storytellers: Voice-Over Narration in American Fiction Film.* Berkeley: University of California Press.

Kuhn, Annette. 1982. *Women's Pictures: Feminism and Cinema.* London: Routledge and Kegan Paul.

———. 1984. "Women's Genres: Melodrama, Soap Opera and Theory." *Screen* 25, no. 1 (Jan./Feb.): 18-28.

Lafaye, Jacques. 1976. *Quetzalcoatl and Guadalupe: The Formation of Mexican National Consciousness, 1531–1813.* Trans. Benjamin Keen. Chicago: University of Chicago Press.

Lamb, Ruth S. 1975. *Mexican Theater of the Twentieth Century.* Claremont, Calif.: Ocelot Press.

Lant, Antonia. 1991. *Blackout: Reinventing Women for Wartime British Cinema.* Princeton: Princeton University Press.

León-Portilla, Miguel, ed. 1992. *The Broken Spears: The Aztec Account of the Conquest of Mexico.* Boston: Beacon Press.

Lévi-Strauss, Claude. 1958. "Introduction: History and Anthropology." In his *Structural Anthropology.* Trans. Claire Jacobson and Brooke Grundfest Schoepf. New York: Basic Books.

———. 1972. "The Structural Study of Myth." In *The Structuralists from Marx to Lévi-Strauss,* ed. Richard de George and Fernande de George. Garden City, N.Y.: Doubleday.

López, Ana M. 1985. "The Melodrama in Latin America: Films, Telenovelas and the Currency of a Popular Form." *Wide Angle* 7, no. 3: 4-13.

———. 1991a. "Celluloid Tears: Melodrama in the 'Old' Mexican Cinema." *Iris: A Journal of Image and Sound* 13 (summer): 29-51.

———. 1991b. "Are All Latins from Manhattan? Hollywood, Ethnography, and Cultural Colonialism." In *Unspeakable Images: Ethnicity and the American Cinema,* ed. Lester D. Friedman. Urbana: University of Illinois Press.

Lowe, Sarah M. 1991. *Frida Kahlo.* New York: Universe.

Maduro, Renaldo J., and Joseph B. Wheelwright. 1992. "Archetype and Archetypal Image." In *Jungian Literary Criticism,* ed. Richard P. Sugg. Evanston, Ill.: Northwestern University Press.

Martín-Barbero, Jesús. 1993. *Communication, Culture and Hegemony: From the Media to Mediations.* Trans. Elizabeth Fox and Robert A. White. London: Sage.

Matthews, J. H. 1971. *Surrealism and Film*. Ann Arbor: University of Michigan Press.

Mayne, Judith. 1988. *Private Novels, Public Films*. Athens: University of Georgia Press.

———. 1989. *Kino and the Woman Question: Feminism and Soviet Silent Film*. Columbus: Ohio State University Press.

Modleski, Tania. 1991. "Cinema and the Dark Continent: Race and Gender in Popular Film." In *Feminism without Women: Culture and Criticism in a "Postfeminist" Age*, ed. Tania Modleski. New York: Routledge.

Monsiváis, Carlos. 1976. "Notas sobre la cultura mexicana en el siglo XX." In *Historia general de Mexico*, vol. 4. Mexico: El Colegio de México, 1976.

———. 1993. "Mexican Cinema: Of Myths and Demystifications." In *Mediating Two Worlds*, ed. John King, Ana M. López, and Manuel Alvarado. London: BFI.

Mora, Carl J. 1989. *Mexican Cinema: Reflections of a Society, 1896–1988*. Rev. ed. Berkeley: University of California Press.

Newton, Judith, and Deborah Rosenfelt. 1985. *Feminist Criticism and Social Change: Sex, Class and Race in Literature and Culture*. New York: Methuen.

Nicholson, Linda J., and Nancy Fraser. 1990. "Social Criticism without Philosophy: An Encounter between Feminism and Postmodernism." In *Feminism/Postmodernism*, ed. Linda J. Nicholson and Nancy Fraser. New York: Routledge.

O'Malley, Ilene V. 1986. *The Myth of the Revolution: Hero Cults and the Institutionalization of the Mexican State, 1920–1940*. Westport, Conn.: Greenwood Press.

Oms, Marcel. 1985. *Don Luis Buñuel*. Paris: Editions du Cerf.

Paz, Octavio. 1985. *The Labyrinth of Solitude*. Trans. Lysander Kemp. New York: Grove Press.

Pescatello, Ann M. 1976. *Power and Pawn: The Female in Iberian Families, Societies, and Cultures*. London: Greenwood Press.

Petro, Patrice. 1989. *Joyless Streets: Women and Representation in Weimar Germany*. Princeton: Princeton University Press.

Place, Janey. 1980. "Women in Film Noir." In *Women in Film Noir*, ed. E. Ann Kaplan. Rev. ed. London: BFI.

Polan, Dana. 1986. *Power and Paranoia: History, Narrative, and the American Cinema, 1940–1950*. New York: Columbia University Press.

Ramirez Berg, Charles. 1989. "The Image of Women in Recent Mexican Cinema." *Journal of Latin American Popular Culture* 8: 157–181.

———. 1992a. *Cinema of Solitude: A Critical Study of Mexican Film, 1967–1983*. Austin: University of Texas Press.

———. 1992b. "Figueroa's Skies and Oblique Perspective: Notes on the Development of the Classical Mexican Style." *Spectator* 13 (spring): 21–41.

Ramos, Samuel. 1962. *Profile of Man and Culture*. Trans. Peter G. Earle. Austin: University of Texas Press. Originally published in 1934.

Rimmon-Kenan, Shlomith. 1983. *Narrative Fiction: Contemporary Poetics*. London: Routledge.

Rivière, Joan. 1966. "Womanliness as a Masquerade." In *Psychoanalysis and Female Sexuality*, ed. Henrick M. Ruitenbeck. New Haven, Conn.: College University Press.

Rodowick, D. N. 1982. "Madness, Authority, and Ideology in the Domestic Melodrama of the 1950s." *The Velvet Light Trap* no. 19: 40–45.

———. 1991. *The Difficulty of Difference: Psychoanalysis, Sexual Difference, and Film Theory.* New York: Routledge.

Rozado, Alejandro. 1991. *Cine y realidad social in México: Una lectura de la obra de Emilio Fernández.* Guadalajara: Universidad de Guadalajara.

Salas, Elizabeth. 1990. *Soldaderas in the Mexican Military: Myth and History.* Austin: University of Texas Press.

Sánchez, Francisco. 1989. *Crónica antisolemne del cine mexicano.* Mexico City: Universidad Veracruzana.

Schatz, Thomas. 1981. *Hollywood Genres: Formulas, Filmmaking, and the Studio System.* New York: Random House.

Schlesinger, Philip. 1987. "On National Identity: Some Conceptions and Misconceptions Criticized." *Social Science Information* 26:219–264.

Schmidt, Henry C. 1978. *The Roots of Lo Mexicano: Self and Society in Mexican Thought, 1900–1943.* College Station: Texas A & M University Press.

Schnitman, Jorge A. 1984. *Film Industries in Latin America: Dependency and Development.* Norwood, N.J.: ABLEX.

Schutte, Ofelia. 1992. *Cultural Identity and Social Liberation in Latin American Thought.* New York: State University of New York Press.

Scott, James C. 1985. *Weapons of the Weak: Everyday Forms of Resistance.* New Haven, Conn.: Yale University Press.

Seton, Marie. 1952. *Sergei M. Eisenstein.* London: Bodley Head.

Shohat, Ella. 1991. "Gender and Culture of Empire: Toward a Feminist Ethnography of the Cinema." *Quarterly Review of Film and Video* 13, nos. 1–3: 45–84.

Singer, Morris. 1969. *Growth, Equality, and the Mexican Experience.* Latin American Monographs, no. 16. Austin: Institute of Latin American Studies, University of Texas.

Sommer, Doris. 1991. *Foundational Fictions: The National Romances of Latin America.* Berkeley: University of California Press.

Soto, Shirlene. 1990. *Emergence of the Modern Mexican Woman: Her Participation in Revolution and Struggle for Equality, 1910–1940.* Denver: Arden Press.

Todorov, Tzvetan. 1984. *The Conquest of America: The Question of the Other.* Trans. Richard Howard. New York: Harper & Row.

Tuñón, Julia. 1988. *En su propio espejo: Entrevista con Emilio "El Indio" Fernández.* Mexico City: Universidad Autónoma Metropolitana-Iztapapalpa.

———. 1992. *Mujeres de luz y sombra: La construcción masculina de una imagen (1939–1952).* 2 vols. Mexico City: UNAM Historia.

———. 1993. "Between the Nation and Utopia: The Image of Mexico in the Films of Emilio 'Indio' Fernández." *Studies in Latin American Popular Culture* 12: 159–174.

BIBLIOGRAPHY

Turim, Maureen. 1989. *Flashbacks in Film: Memory and History.* New York: Routledge.

Turner, Frederick C. 1968. *The Dynamic of Mexican Nationalism.* Chapel Hill: University of North Carolina Press.

de Usabel, Gaiska S. 1982. *The High Noon of American Films in Latin America.* Ann Arbor, Mich.: UMI Research Press.

Vasconcelos, José. 1979. *The Cosmic Race.* Trans. Didier T. Joen. Los Angeles: California State University.

Vasudevan, Ravi. 1989. "The Melodramatic Mode and the Commercial Hindi Cinema." *Screen* 30, no. 3 (summer): 29–50.

Viñas, Moisés. 1992. *Índice cronológico del cine mexicano, 1896–1992.* Mexico City: UNAM.

Warner, Marina. 1985. *Alone of All Her Sex: The Myth and Cult of the Virgin Mary.* London: Picador.

Williams, Linda. 1981. *Figures of Desire: A Theory and Analysis of Surrealist Film.* Berkeley: University of California Press.

―――. 1984. "Something Else besides a Mother: *Stella Dallas* and the Maternal Melodrama." *Cinema Journal* 24, no. 1 (fall): 2–27.

Williams, Raymond. 1977. *Marxism and Literature.* Oxford: Oxford University Press.

Wolf, Eric R. 1959. *Sons of the Shaking Earth.* Chicago: University of Chicago Press.

Wollen, Peter. 1969. "Eisenstein's Aesthetic." In *Signs and Meanings in the Cinema*, ed. Peter Wollen. Bloomington: Indiana University Press.

Wood, Robin. 1986. *Hollywood from Vietnam to Reagan.* New York: Columbia University Press.

―――. 1988. *Hitchcock's Films Revisited.* New York: Columbia University Press.

INDEX

Illustrations are in italics

women (*continued*)
   as female genre, 42; moral reformation and, 71; as positive role models,
   90; social status of, 85, 86; traditional
   values and, 80, 83–84
World War II: Mexican cinematic his-

tory and, 4, 125–126; Mexico in,
138n. 9

Zapata, Emiliano, 25
zarzuelas, 40–41
Zea, Leopoldo, 51

Joanne Hershfield teaches courses on feminism and film, Third World cinema, and film and video production in the Department of Communication Studies at the University of North Carolina at Chapel Hill. Her previous publications include "Assimilation and Identification in *Cabeza de Vaca*," in *Wide Angle*, and "The Construction of 'Woman' in *Distinto amanacer*," in *The Spectator: A Journal of Film and Television*. Another essay, "Paradise Regained: Eisenstein's *Que Viva Mexico!* as Ethnography" is in *Documenting the Documentary*, edited by Barry K. Grant and Jeannette Sloniowksi, from Wayne State University Press. Hershfield is also a film- and videomaker. Her documentary *Between Two Worlds: A Japanese Pilgrimage* won the Bronze Apple at the National Educational Film and Video Festival in 1995.

Professor Hershfield is currently working on a book-length study on stardom and ethnicity in the classical Hollywood cinema. *Dark Star: The Case of Dolores del Río* focuses on the intersection of ethnicity with the already troubling conjunction of stardom and gender within a specific historical context.